STATE LOTTERIES
AND
LEGALIZED GAMBLING

STATE LOTTERIES AND LEGALIZED GAMBLING

Painless Revenue or Painful Mirage

RICHARD McGOWAN

Q

QUORUM BOOKS
Westport, Connecticut • London

Library of Congress Cataloging-in-Publication Data

McGowan, Richard.
   State lotteries and legalized gambling : painless revenue or painful mirage
/ Richard McGowan.
     p. cm.
   Includes bibliographical references and index.
   ISBN 0–89930–859–7 (alk. paper)
   1. Gambling—Government policy—United States. 2. Lotteries—
Government policy—United States. I. Title.
   HV6715.M4   1994
   336.1′7′0973—dc20   94–15884

British Library Cataloguing in Publication Data is available.

Library of Congress Catalog Card Number: 94–15884
ISBN: 0–89930–859–7

First published in 1994

Quorum Books, 88 Post Road West, Westport, CT 06881
An imprint of Greenwood Publishing Group, Inc.

Printed in the United States of America

∞™

The paper used in this book complies with the
Permanent Paper Standard issued by the National
Information Standards Organization (Z39.48–1984).

10 9 8 7 6 5 4 3 2

For my mother and father, who taught me that life
is not worth living unless you are able to take a risk

Contents

Part III. The Future of Lotteries and Legalized Gambling

Acknowledgments

It is interesting to note the reaction of colleagues and friends when you mention that you are writing a book on lotteries and gambling. Most want to know if the book will focus on schemes for "winning." When they are told that the book will be about operational strategies, both in the public and in the business sectors, there is a look of disappointment that quickly turns into amazement. For while they readily acknowledge that this could be a very interesting topic, they want to know, How did you ever get interested in it? The answers lie below.

First, I need to thank Tom O'Heir and Eric Turner, the two directors of the Massachusetts Lottery Commission, under whose tutelage I became increasingly interested in the lottery question. Besides providing me access to enormous amounts of lottery sales data for lotteries not only in the United States but in other countries, they were extremely helpful and open in giving me insights into how they managed their "business" and the political difficulties that they face. Representatives of lotteries from the District of Columbia, Pennsylvania, Rhode Island, and Connecticut were also quite helpful in commenting on my work and giving me additional insights into the workings of their lotteries.

Second, I wish to thank my former students, especially those in my business policy courses at Boston College (BC). They forced me to clarify my views on how to formulate a business strategy for a lottery as well as to delineate the problems that lotteries encounter as they go through the public policy process. There were also a number of former BC students who did yeoman work in gathering and sorting data for me. In particular, I would like to thank Tim Morse and Mark Streeter for "crunching" the lottery sales figures into a manageable form. Ward Winslow was extremely helpful in assembling and condensing the current literature on lotteries, and Nick Donahue did an extremely professional job in providing me information about foreign lotteries.

   I would like to thank Dr. Richard Passon, provost of the University of Scranton, who was very understanding in giving me the time to finish this project. Finally, I would like to acknowledge the Jesuit Communities at both Boston College and the University of Scranton not only for their support of the project but for their patience in letting me talk through many of my ideas with them.

Preface

The current state of the lottery movement in the United States has nearly a thirty-year history, starting with New Hampshire's adoption of a lottery in 1964. As of 1994, there are thirty-eight states along with the District of Columbia (D.C.) that sponsor lotteries. In 1992, these lotteries contributed approximately $11.5 billion to government treasuries. By way of comparison, the contribution that lotteries make to government coffers is slightly over twice what people spend on movie tickets in the United States.

What the above data demonstrate is that the lottery is the vehicle by which government has entered into the entertainment industry. A lottery is a somewhat unique creation insofar that it is a creature of both the public and business policy processes. Certainly, a lottery has to be approved by state legislatures, and the vast majority of lotteries are operated by state commissions that in turn are under the supervision of legislative committees. Yet a lottery has to be viewed as a business that is competing for the entertainment dollars of the public.

The strategy that lottery directors employ to operate their lottery business has to take into account two goals: (1) It must raise sufficient revenue to satisfy the needs of revenue-starved state governments, and (2) at the same time, it must maintain the public "tolerance" of this slightly unsavory method of raising revenue for the state. The purpose of this book is to analyze both the public and business policy processes under which lotteries function in trying to fulfill these two sometimes conflicting goals.

There have been many fine studies written about this recent surge in lottery activity. Nearly all of these works have focused on the various public policy concerns that have been expressed by officials and other stakeholder groups when the lottery question is considered. The primary issues that these books deal with are (1) the "fairness" or equity issue and (2) the "economics" of a lottery as a source of revenue for the state. Charles T. Clotfelter and Philip J. Cook's *Selling Hope: State Lotteries in America* (1989) is an excellent example of a work that examines the "regressivity" of a lottery as a tax. In this work, they conclude that the lottery is "unfair" since it is in actuality a regressive form of taxation aimed at the poor. In *The Economic Consequences of State Lotteries* (1991), Mary O. Borg, Paul M. Mason, and Stephen L. Shapiro conducted a survey of consumer spending on lottery tickets in both Florida and Georgia. These authors were attempting to examine two economic aspects of the lottery: the equity issue as well as the efficiency of raising government revenues using a lottery. Their results seem to be inconclusive. Alan J. Karcher's *Lotteries* (1989) provides a fascinating review of the various issues that public policy makers face when they are considering instituting as well as maintaining a lottery. Karcher was speaker of the New Jersey General Assembly during much of the debate about New Jersey's involvement in a lottery, and he provides a fascinating "insider's" view of the process as well as comments on the many potential pitfalls that state officials face as they determine how to conduct their lotteries. There are, of course, numerous other studies and journal articles that examine these public policy concerns, yet curiously, there is nothing written about formulating and implementing strategies for operating a state lottery.

The intention of this volume is not to duplicate any of this previous work. The book is divided into three parts (much like Caesar's Gaul!). Part I, consisting of three chapters, focuses on the public policy process. Chapter 1 provides the reader with a brief history of lotteries in the United States. It asserts that the public's tolerance of lottery activity can be correlated with the financing of wars. Chapter 2 reviews the worldwide lottery situation. There is a brief description of how lotteries began and how they are currently being operated in countries ranging from Spain to China. This chapter emphasizes the similarities and dissimilarities between operations of American and foreign lotteries. Chapter 3 summarizes the various ethical arguments that public policy officials must analyze from both advocates as well as opponents of lotteries and state-sponsored gambling. These positions are characterized as the "ethics of sacrifice" and the "ethics of tolerance."

Part II addresses the various business policy issues that lottery directors face as they are trying to determine what strategies they need to employ to meet the goals of public policy makers. Chapter 4 attempts to answer the question of whether a lottery can be a consistent source of revenue for a state. In order to do this, the strategies that states employ in conducting their lotteries need to be analyzed to determine which games—or combination of games—provide a steady stream of revenue for state treasuries. Chapter 5 deals with the phenomenon of states that are greatly expanding the type and amount of legalized state-sponsored gambling. To increase gambling revenue, states are permitting keno gambling, video poker games, offtrack betting (OTB), video lottery, and riverboat gambling as well as casino gambling. Using ARIMA (autoregressive integrated moving average) intervention time series analysis, this chapter determines whether or not the introduction of these new forms of gambling "cannibalizes" existing lottery sales. Chapter 6 compares and contrasts the overall gambling strategies of Massachusetts and Pennsylvania. These case studies illustrate how the business of operating a lottery and other forms of gambling both influences and is influenced by the public policy process.

Part III provides the reader with a view of the future of lotteries and other forms of legalized gambling in the United States. Chapter 7 deals with the "privatization" of gambling. It appears that as gambling "stakes" are being raised by public policy makers, the risk of failure will also go up. To avoid this risk, state governments will allow private entrepreneurs to operate these riskier gambling ventures such as casino and riverboat gambling. The state's role will be as regulator, although the state still stands to profit greatly from these additional gambling activities. This chapter proposes a model to evaluate whether this privatization of gambling can be termed *successful*. Chapter 8 contains a series of strategic alternatives from which public policy officials can choose in order to determine what the proper overall gambling strategy ought to be for their states. This chapter and the book conclude by commenting on the lessons that this explosion in lottery and gambling activity can teach us about the current state of public and business policy in the United States.

PART I

LOTTERIES: HISTORY, CONTROVERSIES, AND CURRENT STATE

Chapter 1

The Three Waves of Lottery Activity in the United States

Gambling is an activity that has existed from the beginning of civilization. Many proponents of gambling justify it on the grounds that it is a civilized way of satisfying the human need to take a "risk." Yet gambling has never been looked on as a completely desirable activity. The Greeks use the following myth to express their ambivalence to gambling: Tyche, the goddess of good luck, was seduced by Zeus. The daughter who resulted from this illicit union was a mischievous tormentor of human beings. She seduced ordinary mortals into playing various games of chance and thoroughly enjoyed the misery that they inflicted on the losers.

The Romans were much more enthusiastic gamblers. The Circus Maximus, which had a seating capacity of 380,000, was the site of some fifty chariot races every day. Yet even the Romans were leery of promoting gambling too much. The Latin for gambler, *aleator,* was considered a derisive term, and Roman law failed to consider any gambling wager as an enforceable contract (i.e., the winner could not sue a loser for his or her winnings in a Roman court of law).

For the ancient Jew, gambling was also an activity that was reserved to only the "seamier" parts of society. Known gamblers were not permitted to testify in Jewish courts, for it was thought that gamblers' testimony could be bought in order to pay off their gambling debts. In addition, if a Jew won from a fellow Jew, those winnings not only had to be returned, but they had to be paid back double; if a Jew had won from a Gentile, the winnings did not have to be returned, although the Jewish gambler would still receive some small punishment (Fleming, 1978, p. 130).

For strict Muslims, gambling is absolutely forbidden in any form. The Koran states: "Satan seeks to sow dissension and hatred among you by means of wine and lots . . . therefore abstain from them." It is interesting to note that although casino gambling is legal in Muslim Egypt, Egyptian nationals are barred from entering these casinos, and all patrons must produce a valid foreign passport.

As a result of its unsavory reputation, restrictions on gambling have been adopted by practically every country in the world throughout history. The usual legal scenario involves outlawing casino gambling (unless the area is hoping to attract tourists, especially those who are considered "outsiders") as well as most other forms of gambling but to permit and sponsor lotteries and horse racing, which are considered the "harmless" forms of gambling.

The current controversy in the United States about lotteries and government's role in the gambling industry is merely a continuation of a debate that began in the 1600s with the founding of colonial America. This debate has always contained both economic and political elements that cannot be addressed separately. For the question that public policy officials face when they are dealing with the lottery question and gambling in general is: Does the revenue from the lottery or gambling justify the state's "tolerance" of this "necessary evil"? In other words, even proponents of lotteries or gambling generally concede that it is not a "good" activity but one that can be used to fund "good" causes.

This chapter will catalog the various episodes or distinct "waves" of lottery activity (as well as other gambling activities) in the history of the United States. The term *wave* is used to illustrate the rather cyclical and repetitive nature of intense lottery activity in U.S. history. For each wave, there will be a description of the good "causes" that lotteries supported as well as the circumstances that led to the eventual demise of intense lottery activity. See Table

Table 1.1
Three Waves of Lottery Activity

Wave	Cause (War)	Beneficiaries	Operator	Types of Games	Causes of Decline
First wave: 1607 - 1820	Revolutionary War	Continental Army Colleges Capital projects Private charities	Private brokers licensed by individual states	Lotteries and onetime sweepstakes	Scandals - fraud by operators New, more stable revenue resources such as excise taxes
Second wave: 1868 - 1895	Civil War	Southern states - primarily Louisiana supporting: rebuilding roads, infrastructure	Private brokers licensed by states	Weekly drawings Weekly mailings National in scope	Scandals in Louisiana Legislature Nationwide protest over use of mails for gambling
Third wave: 1964 - present	Cold War	38 states and D.C. supporting: education, health, transportation	State operated although a few states have "privatized"	Daily numbers Instant games Lotto games Keno Video poker OTB Sport betting Casinos	No state has abandoned any lottery instituted since 1964

1.1 for a summary of these waves of lottery activity. Finally, there will also be a description of how lotteries were operated during each of these waves of lottery activity. Hopefully, the similarities and differences between each of the waves will be able to shed some light on why the lottery has been such an attractive option for public policy makers throughout U.S. history.

FIRST WAVE (1607–1820)

The first settlers at Jamestown, Virginia, endured almost every conceivable type of hardship as they settled the New World and the merchants financing this adventure faced financial disaster. To support their Jamestown venture, the settlers petitioned the English Parliament to conduct a lottery in England.

However, this was a time when England was awash in lotteries sponsored both by the government and by private concerns. In 1620, the House of Commons ordered the Virginia Company to stop selling tickets since the company's lotteries were competing with government lotteries that were not bringing in the amount of revenue that legislators had expected. With this major source of revenue for the colony drying up, the colony's sufferings increased all the more (Sullivan, 1972, p. 14).

What this incident illustrates quite clearly is that playing lottery games came as naturally to English colonists as drinking tea. Although this initial lottery could be classified as a failure, it certainly did not dissuade fellow colonists from starting lotteries once they settled on American shores. In fact, lottery activity continued to increase steadily until the Revolutionary War, after which there was a virtual explosion in lottery activity for fifty years. It was not until the 1840s that almost all states outlawed lotteries.

The purpose of this section is to examine why lotteries were such a popular source of government funding during this period of time. Since it appears that the Revolutionary War was a watershed event in early American lottery activity, this section will be divided into two parts: pre–Revolutionary War and post–Revolutionary War.

Pre–Revolutionary War Lottery Activity

Lotteries were held throughout the early 1700s for all kinds of "good" causes that can be classified into two categories: educational institutions and public interest projects. The breakdown of good causes for lottery activity ought to give the reader a feel for the type of lottery activity that was tolerated during the early development of the United States.

Educational Institutions. One of the chief beneficiaries of lottery activity during the early 1700s was the developing American educational system. These educational lotteries had a twofold pur-

pose: (1) to fund building projects for the struggling higher education institutions and (2) to establish basic education in frontier
areas.

One of the first colleges to use lotteries to fund building projects
was the College of Philadelphia (later known as the University of
Pennsylvania). During the early 1700s, this institution conducted
nine different lotteries for various building enterprises. But the
future University of Pennsylvania had much company in using lotteries as the primary method of financing its building projects.

Both Yale and Harvard College (even in the earliest days, these
two institutions aped each other!) used lotteries to build dormito-
ries. In 1747, the Connecticut legislature gave Yale a license to
raise £7,500, while Harvard waited until 1765 to win approval
from the Massachusetts legislature to conduct a lottery worth
£3,200. It is interesting to note that Harvard's fund-raising lottery
was much less successful than Yale's lottery. The primary reason
for the failure of Harvard's lottery was that it had to compete with
lotteries that were being operated to support the troops that were
fighting the French and Indian War. However, it certainly appears
that Harvard has learned from its past mistakes, and its timing for
fund-raising has greatly improved! But there were many other
now-famous higher educational institutions that received their initial financial impetus from operating lotteries.

In 1746, King's College (later known as Columbia) sought a
license from New York State to raise £2,250 for classroom buildings. This was the first of five lotteries that King's College would
run until 1755. The New York legislature was also asked to authorize a lottery to benefit Union College. Rival Columbia objected
heatedly to this competition; so to appease Columbia, the New
York legislature gave Columbia a twenty-one-acre tract of land
that included the land on which Rockefeller Center is built. Obviously, this source of revenue for Columbia was far greater than any
lottery or series of lotteries could have ever raised for that institution.

In marked contrast to Columbia's hostilely opposing a rival's
ability to raise funds through lottery activity, other colleges and

states were remarkably charitable in permitting lotteries to benefit other colleges. For example, the College of New Jersey (later known as Princeton) petitioned the New Jersey legislature for permission to operate a lottery. However, the New Jersey state legislature refused to give college officials permission to have lottery drawings. But the Connecticut assembly, which was dominated by Yale graduates, did permit the College of New Jersey to conduct its lottery on its territory. One can only hope that Princeton graduates recall this largesse of Yale graduates! Massachusetts officials were also quite generous in allowing lottery tickets for the benefit of Dartmouth to be sold within its borders during this early colonial period. Perhaps the Harvard graduates in the Massachusetts legislature were aware of Harvard's failed attempt with a lottery and did not think that the little college to the north could successfully operate a lottery. However, Massachusetts residents were much more sympathetic to Dartmouth's needs than they were to Harvard's, and the Dartmouth lottery was a success.

Other levels of education also benefited from lottery activity. In Georgia, nearly twenty lotteries were operated to build and fund county "academies," one-room schoolhouses that later became the foundation of the public school system in Georgia. Other states such as Mississippi, Kentucky, and North Carolina and many others permitted lotteries so that local communities could raise sufficient funds to build schoolhouses. Hence, in many ways, lotteries made a significant contribution to the funding and development of the early American education system.

Public Interest Projects. This category includes a number of "causes" that benefited either individuals, institutions, or society as a whole. Lotteries were used to raise funds to finance new businesses such as hemp growing in New York and paper manufacturing in Massachusetts. Individuals were also routinely given permission to conduct lotteries if the proceeds of the lottery were used to pay the debts of a person who had gone bankrupt and was put in prison until he could pay his debts. While this might sound like an extreme example, it was not an unusual incident during this wave of lottery activity.

Thomas Jefferson was a staunch advocate of using lotteries to raise public funds. He called them a "salutary instrument wherein the tax is laid on the willing only" (Fleming, 1978, p. 32). In 1826, the eighty-three-year-old former president had to apply to the Virginia legislature for permission to operate a lottery for himself. The United States was in the throes of a severe economic depression, with land and crop prices falling, and so most of the wealthy landowners in the South were experiencing financial difficulties.

Jefferson cosigned a promissory note of $20,000 for a friend even though he himself was already in debt $80,000. When his friend defaulted, they demanded that Jefferson pay the money. The only assets that Jefferson had were his home and two other parcels of Virginia real estate. However, the price that Jefferson would receive for his properties would not cover his debts. He decided that the best way to raise money was to initiate a lottery that would use his landholdings as the chief prize. The lottery was never carried out because Jefferson died on July 4, 1826, a few months before the lottery was to have taken place.

Lotteries were operated in New York for the Relief of Poor Widows and in Pennsylvania for the "useful arts." New Jersey permitted lotteries to help pay for a church steeple and to build boat landings. Massachusetts supported several lotteries in the 1760s to rebuild Faneuil Hall, which had been gutted by a fire. In many ways, colonial lotteries were today's equivalent of a state's permission for nonprofit institutions to issue nontaxable bonds. Lotteries were an essential form of financing public projects for colonial governments since their ability to levy taxes was always being attacked. Every colony and almost every citizen had experience with lotteries that muted any opposition to lottery activity.

Post–Revolutionary War Lottery Activity

With the coming of the Revolutionary War, the number of lotteries and the causes that lotteries supported greatly expanded. The two good causes (educational institutions and nonprofit activities) that had previously been financed by lottery activity continued to use lotteries as a means of finance. However, with the occurrence of the Revolutionary War, two other causes were added to the list that used lotteries as a means of support—namely, financing the Revolutionary War itself and building the country's transportation system.

Financing the Revolutionary War. While the British redcoats certainly provided an ample military threat to the newly declared independent colonies, perhaps the greatest problem that the Continental Congress faced was finding the money to finance the war. Taxation was out of the question. Since the colonists had been provoked into declaring their independence because of their deep-seated hatred of taxation of any kind or form, public officials were well aware that imposing taxes on the population was certainly not in their best interest.

In order to pay for the war effort, Congress would do three things: (1) It would issue paper, which would eventually lead to rampant inflation; (2) it would borrow money from foreign powers such as France, Spain, and Holland, all of whom did contribute substantially to the Revolutionary War cause; and (3) it would establish a national lottery, which was the most politically painless way to raise funds. On November 1, 1776, the Board of the Treasury announced its plan to establish this national lottery, and with the institution of this lottery, lottery mania raged throughout all of the colonies.

The goal of the national lottery was to raise $1,005,000 for the Continental Army. While this goal was not met, it provided the basis for almost every colony to hold a lottery in support of its troops. In 1778, Massachusetts sought to raise $750,000 to entice enlistments into its army and held another lottery later to fund the $20,400 it needed to clothe its army. Many other states such as New York, Vermont, Rhode Island, North and South Carolina, and Virginia also held lotteries in support of their Revolutionary War forces. But this explosion in lottery activity did not end with the conclusion of the war.

Public Projects. The decades after the Revolutionary War were ones of great population growth. From 1790 to 1810, New York's population grew from 340,120 to 959,049. In this same period,

Kentucky's population grew from 73,677 to 406,511, while Pennsylvania's population went from 434,373 to 810,081. There was very similar growth in population for all of the other former colonies.

If these state governments had to provide just the same services that they were providing before the Revolutionary War, this in itself would have forced these governments to find additional sources of revenue. But besides providing additional services to accommodate this explosive population growth, the citizens of these states were also demanding that the state provide for the capital improvements necessary to sustain economic growth. Again, lotteries were viewed as the politically painless method of raising revenue to satisfy the public's desire for social improvements.

The biggest sums raised by lotteries during this post–Revolutionary War period went toward building up the internal infrastructure of the nation. As the population increased and moved westward, roads and bridges had to be constructed and canals built.

Roads such as Mountain Road that connected the Ohio River with Virginia and canals such as the Erie Canal were needed to spur commerce. Massachusetts granted lottery authorizations for projects such as building bridges that would connect Ipswich and Gloucester (north of Boston) and another that would cross the Connecticut River so that farm produce and textile products could reach Connecticut from the Springfield area. In Pennsylvania, lotteries raised $400,000 for various capital projects. This money was used to construct canals between the Schuykill and Delaware Rivers and between the Schuykill and Susquehanna Rivers. Lotteries were the source of funding for most of the great canals that were built during the early 1800s, the great canal-building era.

There were also a variety of other capital projects that used lotteries as a means of financing these worthy causes. Frankfort, Kentucky, was authorized to conduct a lottery to raise $50,000 for a water supply. Both St. Louis and Detroit were permitted to have lotteries by their respective states in order to finance fire-fighting equipment. Once again, educational institutions needed to expand and develop, and they again turned to lotteries to support this cause.

When it was finally agreed that the new nation needed a capital, Congress launched a lottery in order to pay for it. This national lottery was a great success but was greatly opposed by the states who were also conducting lotteries at the same time. It certainly was a precursor of competition between federal officials and state officials over various ways of raising revenue. Once again, lotteries proved to be the tried and proven method to raise funds for these projects, and about one hundred lotteries were conducted in the ten-year period at the end of the Revolutionary War and hundreds of other lotteries were operated during the period from 1810 to 1840.

However, this "golden age" of the lottery lasted only until the 1840s. There were two developments that led to the decline in lottery activity. First, with the passage of the U.S. Constitution, there was finally a strong central government that could and would collect tax revenue. Even those citizens who opposed taxation conceded that if government was to provide needed services, then government must possess a more consistent source of revenue than merely operating lotteries. It is somewhat ironic that the first tax revenues imposed were those on the consumption of whiskey, which sparked the Whiskey Rebellion. But this rebellion was put down and provided legislators the opportunity to impose taxes and collect on them. It also established the American custom of taxing "sin" and enshrining the adage "The wages of sin is a tax." Another factor that made government less dependent on lotteries was the establishment of a reliable financial system. Now state government had the ability to issue bonds in order to pay for needed capital improvements.

But the primary reason why lotteries declined was the method employed to sell lottery tickets. A broker would, first, contact the state or an institution that the state had licensed to conduct a lottery. This broker would point out to those in charge of the lottery that because of his experience and the size of his operation, he could sell a far greater number of tickets than if they attempted to conduct the lottery themselves. The broker was usually paid a percentage of the total amount realized through lottery ticket sales. But this method of payment tempted lottery brokers to sell all sorts of bogus tickets and to engage in all types of illegal schemes. Scandal after scandal broke about lottery fraud, which eventually infuriated the public and forced legislators to abolish lotteries in their states.

The following examples of the corruption that led to the downfall of lottery activity occurred throughout the United States. In 1818, after local newspapers had informed their readers that the Medical Science Lottery was fixed, the New York legislature launched an investigation. The legislature's investigation revealed that the operators regularly informed prominent people, mostly politicians, what the winning numbers would be. After this lottery scandal, public opinion forced New York legislators to enact legislation that banned the sale of lottery tickets in New York.

The scandal surrounding the lottery for Washington, D.C., provoked an outcome that frightened lawmakers all over the country. In 1823, Congress authorized the Grand National Lottery in order to pay for improvements to the city. Tickets were sold, and the drawing took place, but before anyone could collect their winnings, the agent who organized the lottery for D.C. fled town. With him went several hundred thousand dollars that had been awarded as prizes.

While the majority of winners of this lottery accepted their fate with resignation, the winner of the $100,000 grand prize decided to pursue his dream. He sued the District of Columbia, claiming that the city was responsible for the conduct of its agent. The case went all the way to the Supreme Court, where the Court ruled that indeed the city was responsible for the agent's action and therefore obligated to pay him.

This Supreme Court decision was a sobering reminder to local officials that authorizing lotteries could be potentially dangerous and that the proceeds from lotteries were not necessarily painless. With the coming of this potential legal liability along with the public's outcry over various other lottery scandals, the movement to ban lotteries had begun.

During the period from 1840 to 1860, all but two states (Missouri and Kentucky) prohibited lottery activity. In fact, two states (Texas and California) that were admitted to the Union during this period actually had provisions in their constitutions banning lotteries. So in less than a half century, lottery activity rose to new heights and fell just as rapidly. However, while it appeared that lotteries had disappeared, it would take less than thirty years for lotteries to once again explode on the national scene.

SECOND WAVE (1868–1895)

The second period of gambling expansion also coincides with financing another war, namely, the Civil War. Once again, government at all levels was faced with paying for a war that was not overwhelmingly popular and that was devastating to the economy. The victorious North was in no mood to lend either materials or funds to rebuild the South. So in order to raise the money it needed to start the reconstruction process, the Southern states turned to an old friend, namely, lotteries. In the early part of Reconstruction, when carpetbaggers from the North were helping to set up weak state governments, a lottery was perhaps the only method for these unpopular governments to finance any capital improvements. But with the return of stronger state governments, the need to conduct lotteries lessened greatly throughout the South.

The most famous and long-lasting of these Southern Reconstruction lotteries was the Louisiana lottery. This lottery, known as the Serpent, was given to two private brokers, John Morris and Charles Howard, who hired two former Confederate generals, Pierre Gustave Toutant Beauregard and Jubal Anderson Early, to preside over the drawings. There were two aspects to this lottery that were groundbreaking. First, the size of the lottery was enormous. More than $3 million was distributed to winners annually, while profits for the brokers averaged between $3 and $5 million. Second, it was truly the first national lottery held on a weekly basis. By the early 1880s, the other Southern states had given up on their lotteries completely, whereas lotteries were outlawed in the North. Louisiana lottery tickets were hawked in every major city of the United States.

The lottery was immensely popular in Louisiana. Proceeds from the lottery were used to build the first waterworks in New Orleans as well as to support the New Orleans Charity Hospital. Proceeds from this lottery were also used to clean up New Orleans after it was struck with floods in 1890.

Also in 1890, the charter that had been used to authorize the Serpent was within three years of expiring. One of the Serpent's founders, John Morris, offered to give the state $500,000 per year for the next twenty-five years if the charter was renewed. The money would be used to finance a series of levees along the Mississippi. When the governor of Louisiana denounced this offering as a bribe, Morris upped the ante to $1 million a year.

The rather flagrant method that Morris and his associates were employing in order to ensure that the Serpent's charter would be renewed was reported throughout the country. Various state legislatures throughout the country passed resolutions calling on the Congress and president to stop this lottery. There can be little doubt that what upset these legislatures most was the fact that out-of-state sales of Louisiana lottery tickets amounted to over $5 million per year. President Benjamin Harrison urged Congress to pass legislation to curb all lottery activity. The primary piece of legislation that would cripple the Louisiana lottery was to deny the operators of the lottery the use of the federal mails. At the height of the Louisiana lottery's existence, nearly 50 percent of all mail coming into New Orleans was connected to the lottery. If customers could no longer mail in their requests, then the lottery's life would be short-lived. Late in 1890, Congress passed President Harrison's request for legislation. By 1895, the Louisiana lottery had vanished, and as the new century dawned, virtually all lottery activity had ceased to exist. But like a phoenix, the lottery as a method to raise governmental revenue would again be resurrected.

THIRD WAVE (1964–PRESENT)

In 1964, New Hampshire became the first state to operate a lottery in almost seventy years. There was almost overwhelming voter support of this initiative. For New Hampshire voters, the choice was simply: Either approve the lottery, or the state will have to institute a sales or income tax to pay for services. Projections of revenue from this lottery depended greatly on the ability of New Hampshire lottery officials to attract bettors from nearby states such as Massachusetts, Connecticut, and New York. Once again, citizens were rebelling against what they perceived as unnecessarily high taxation, and government turned to lotteries as a painless way of providing relief to its citizens.

It should come as no surprise that two of the states (New York and Massachusetts) whose residents New Hampshire was hoping to attract became the next states to adopt a lottery. Throughout the 1970s, there was a slow but steady adoption of lotteries, mostly by northeastern states.

However, in the 1980s, there was a virtual explosion in lottery activity. Of the thirty-eight lotteries currently being operated in the United States, over 75 percent of them were started after 1980. While the lottery was always a tempting source of revenue for states before 1980, there was always enough resistance to stop the implementation of a lottery. There appear to be two plausible explanations for this sudden surge in lottery popularity: (1) the Reagan cold war financing policy and (2) a change in the prevailing ethic under which public policy officials conduct policy—"the triumph of the ethics of tolerance." This first explanation will be the focus of the rest of this chapter, while the second explanation will be the subject material for Chapter 3.

As with the first two waves of gambling, the high point of this third wave of gambling also coincided with a war, namely, the cold war. In many ways, this was a much more costly war (not of course in terms of human life but certainly in terms of resources expended) than the other two previous wars that have been mentioned. It was a struggle that lasted almost forty years and diverted countless tax dollars to defense spending. In 1980, with the coming of the Reagan administration, there was a concerted effort to "win" this war. The strategy that was employed was simply to outspend the Soviet Union and force its submission on economic grounds. While it was a successful strategy, it did have a cost.

To pay for this military buildup, the federal government was running out of funds that it could use to finance basic functions, such as education and health care. The solution to this problem was known as the "New Federalism." This policy sought to shift the burden of paying for social welfare services to the states, where voters could decide what was the appropriate level of benefits. Thus, with the institution of the Reagan policies, there was a 45 percent rise in the defense budget and a 13 percent decrease in the amount of state and local aid (Karcher, 1989, p. 21).

At the end of this cold war, taxpayers were expecting some relief from the perceived high tax burden that they had been subjected to throughout the cold war period. Yet government at all levels was, and still is, running high deficits. At the federal level, the reduction of the deficit has become one of the primary political goals. Meanwhile, state governments are saddled with social programs (such as Medicare and welfare, even education expenses) that had been initially supported by the federal government but had that support removed as a result of the federal government trying to reduce its own deficit.

Bowing to the public's resistance to any new tax increases, states have, once again, turned to lotteries to provide necessary income for state services. For example, proceeds from California's lottery are used to finance education expenses throughout the state. Supporters of the lottery used education as the "good" cause for lottery proceeds after the passage of the famous Proposition 13. Since Proposition 13 limited any increase in property taxes, and property taxes were the primary method of financing education in California, the lottery became the alternative to raising property taxes in California as well as many other states when the Proposition 13 craze hit other states. In many ways, the current wave of lottery activity in the United States is a mere continuation of a historical trend—that is, lotteries become a means of finance for state governments when they can no longer demand that citizens pay more taxes in order to provide governmental expected services. Yet there also appear to be some profound differences between this wave of the lottery and the two previous waves of U.S. lottery activity.

Table 1.1 reveals four quite pronounced differences between this third wave of gambling and the two previous waves of gambling. First, there is the *breadth* or the widespread use of gambling as a source of revenue for state governments. Thirty-eight states plus the District of Columbia sponsor a lottery. It is somewhat ironic to note that the South is the only section of the country that has so far withstood the lottery craze, but it is also the section of the country that spends the least amount of tax dollars on social and welfare projects.

Second, the *depth* of gambling taking place is unprecedented. No longer is lottery play being confined to a monthly or even a weekly drawing. Most states are offering three types of lottery games. First, there is a daily number game. This game involves selecting a three- or four-digit number for a fixed-amount prize. The second type of game goes under the general rubric of "lotto." This game involves picking six numbers of a possible forty or forty-eight numbers. The game is usually played twice a week, and jackpots can build up quite enormously, sometimes up to $90 million. The final lottery innovation was the "instant" or scratch tickets. In all of these games, the player knows immediately if he or she has won. Also, the odds and the size of the prize for these games can vary greatly. The other striking feature of this third wave is willingness of states to become engaged in other types of gambling activities, such as keno, video poker, offtrack betting (OTB), sports betting, and casino gambling. These developments will be examined further in Chapters 5 and 6.

Another difference between the third and the two previous waves of lottery activity deals with the good causes that lottery proceeds are used to support. In the two previous waves, the good causes that lottery profits supported were one-time events. In the first and second waves, lottery proceeds supported the building of canals, waterworks, bridges, and highways. Once the good cause was completed, then the lottery ceased to exist. While the state needed the lottery to finance these projects, it did not depend on lottery proceeds to fund services that constituents expected the state to provide daily. In this third wave in which the United States presently finds itself, the causes that lottery proceeds support are activities that the state has traditionally funded and that the public expects the state to continue to fund. As was pointed out earlier, California uses lottery proceeds to fund educational expenses; and many other states such as Illinois, Florida, and New Jersey also use lottery proceeds to fund education. Note that these funds are not "supplements" to build new schools and the like but are used for the day-to-day operations of the schools. In other states, lottery proceeds are used to fund Medicare (Pennsylvania) and to support police and fire departments in local communities (Massachusetts) as well as hosts of other day-to-day operations of government.

The present format of state lotteries is no longer a "one-shot" affair. These lotteries must be able to provide the state with a consistent source of revenue in order to fund the various good causes that their supporters insist that they can. Chapter 4 will examine just how "consistent" a source of revenue these lottery games can be.

The final difference between the current wave of lottery activity and previous waves of lottery activity is not only state sponsorship but state ownership of the lottery operations. In the two previous waves of lottery activity, the actual operation of the lottery itself was given to private brokers. But in the current wave of lottery activity, the state itself is the operator and sole beneficiary of lotteries. While some states such as Georgia, Nebraska, West Virginia, and Maine have permitted private concerns such as Scientific Games and G-Tech to operate the instant game portion of their lotteries, the vast majority of lottery operations are conducted by the state itself.

State ownership and operation of lotteries certainly appear to be supported by the historical evidence given in this chapter. There can be little doubt that the downfall of the previous waves of lottery activity was due in great measure to the scandal-ridden operations of the private brokers who were commissioned by the state to operate the lotteries. However, even state-operated lotteries are hardly immune to scandals. Pennsylvania's lottery experienced a major scandal with its daily number drawing in the early 1980s when a daily number drawing was rigged by making the balls heavier than the other balls, with the famous winning number 666.

How long this "exclusive" state ownership of lotteries will last remains to be seen. But as states seek to raise more and more revenue via lottery and other types of gambling, it certainly appears that the state will begin to relinquish control of its monopoly on gambling and will begin to privatize gambling. Chapter 7 will examine this privatization of gambling and will develop a model by which public policy makers can measure a successful privatization.

CONCLUSION

This chapter has illustrated that every wave (or substantial increase) of lottery activity in U.S. history can be correlated with the conduct of a long, costly war. This correlation has the following explanation: to pay for a war that is experiencing waning public support, government officials decide to institute a lottery so that they can avoid raising taxes as well as the issue of whether to continue the struggle. For the lottery is rarely used to finance the war directly; rather, proceeds from the lottery are used to finance needed social services or projects. While even supporters of the lottery would concede that a lottery is not an ideal method of raising revenue, a lottery is "tolerated" by the public as long as it spares them from new taxes and its proceeds support a "good" end.

The first two waves of lottery ended when government officials could no longer demonstrate to the public that a lottery was able to support a good cause and when scandals concerning the lottery outweighed any good it could achieve, so that the lottery was no longer tolerated. Hence, the survival of a lottery depends on two factors:

1. Can a lottery raise sufficient revenue on a consistent basis in order to avoid tax increases?
2. How long will the public tolerate an activity that is considered, at best, amoral by most of the public?

In trying to determine what the fate of the current third wave of lottery activity will be, these two questions need to be addressed.

The question of whether the lottery, along with other forms of gambling, can be a consistent source of revenue for the state will be a topic of extensive analysis in Chapters 4 through 6. It is in this section of the book where the various business strategies for operating a lottery will be examined, along with various diversification strategies so that the revenue stream from lotteries and other gambling activities will be constant.

However, to understand why lottery officials employ the various types of business strategies in conducting their lotteries, one cannot forget that a lottery is as much a political and social question as an economic concern. It should be apparent that the revenue and tolerance questions cannot be separated. The strategy that lottery officials adopt in operating their lotteries is obviously influenced by the amount and type of gambling that the public will tolerate.

The next two chapters will focus on this tolerance issue. Chapter 2 will describe how lotteries are operated throughout the world and how lottery activity is supported in various cultures. This review of lottery activity as a worldwide phenomenon will also enable the reader to view the similarities and differences between the United States and other countries in how they operate their lotteries and other gambling enterprises. Chapter 3 will catalog the various ethical arguments that are used to both support and oppose lotteries as well as forms of gambling. This chapter will also contrast the public policy fortunes of two controversial issues, namely, the smoking and gambling issues. It will show how this concept of political tolerance has been critical in the current resolutions of these two controversial issues.

Chapter 2

Lotteries and Gambling as Worldwide Phenomena

Legalized state-sponsored gambling is in no way a uniquely American phenomenon. Throughout the world, governments not only operate lotteries, but they also maintain and sponsor many other forms of gambling. The global lottery industry alone accounted for total spending at the consumer level of approximately $80 billion in 1992 (TLF, 1993, p. 11). See Table 2.1 for a breakdown of lottery operations in various parts of the world. The purpose of this chapter is to briefly catalog a few examples of other state-sponsored gambling in other countries. The similarities as well as the differences between these foreign and American gambling operations will be highlighted.

The first part of this chapter will briefly describe the lottery and other gambling operations by sampling a few of the many countries that operate lotteries as well as other forms of gambling throughout the world. These countries include Spain, France, Russia, China, Ireland, and Great Britain. A few smaller nations (Albania, Poland, and Indonesia) will also be presented in light of unique issues they face. What is most remarkable about this lottery and gambling phenomenon is that the number of countries that do not operate a lottery is extremely small. For example, every European nation has (or will have) one in place. The nations that were chosen were

Table 2.1
1992 World Lottery Sales (in millions of U.S. dollars)

Region	Lotto	Spiel	Daily #	Sweepstakes	Instant #	Toto	Totals
Africa	$ 75	$ 0	$ 78	$ 121	$ 52	$ 105	$ 431
Australia, Asia & Middle East	2,228	35	1,860	5,983	1,324	296	11,786
Europe	15,021	1,223	591	8,524	6,208	5,883	37,450
North America	10,711	301	7,487	1,298	8,349	169	28,314
Central America South America	244	0	218	505	227	261	1,455
Overall Totals	28,279	1,559	10,234	16,431	16,160	6,714	79,436

Source: "Breakdown of Lottery Sales Worldwide," 1993 World Lottery Almanac, Terri LaFleur Publications.

selected on the basis of size, major issues, and the availability of information about them.

With this rudimentary understanding of the operational features and major issues in these countries in place, the second section of this chapter will summarize some similarities and dissimilarities between American and foreign lottery and gambling operations. This summary will provide the reader with insights about the future of the gambling industry in the United States.

SPAIN

The Spanish have long been avid gamblers, and lotteries have been available to them for centuries. The Spanish lottery was introduced by King Carlos III in 1763 and has been used to finance such ventures as the Napoleonic War in 1811 (*The Times of London*, December 22, 1992).

Spain is second only to the United States in terms of total gambling expenditures. In 1987, approximately $21.9 billion was spent (see Figure 2.1).

Figure 2.1
Distribution of Gambling in Spain, 1987

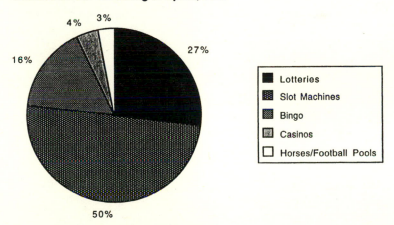

Source: *The Economist*, January 16, 1988

Besides the national lottery, another is run by ONCE (Organi-zación Nacional de Ciegos), a national organization for the blind. Perhaps the best-known lottery in Spain, however, is the nationally administered *El Gordo* ("The Fat One"), which is held annually a few days before Christmas.

The National Lottery

The Organismo Nacional de Loterías y Apuestas del Estado (ONLAE) operates the national lottery. Most games are of stan-dard "numbers" with three draws per week. Over 8 million peo-ple played the lottery games per week in 1991, bringing in revenues in excess of $5.9 billion for that year (*El Pais,* May 31, 1992).

The revenues for the lottery games are managed by three banks. Bank Argentina manages revenues from the games *Primitiva* and *Bobo Loto* and football polls everywhere except in Madrid. This amounts to $90 million per year. Banco Bilbao Viczaya manages the *Lotería Nacional* game, approximately $240 million per year. Finally, Caja Madrid manages all games in Madrid, approximately $100 million per year.

The Spanish treasury receives a relatively small amount of these revenues. In 1991, it only received $1.7 billion, while charities, particularly the Red Cross, received $84 million.

El Gordo

The world's largest (in terms of payout) and oldest lottery is Spain's *El Gordo* ("The Fat One"). It is a five-digit numbers game held only once a year, a few days before Christmas.

El Gordo is regarded in Spain as "more popular than Santa Claus," with each of Spain's 39 million people spending an aver-age of $48 on it every year (*Chicago Tribune,* December 23, 1992). The annual drawing is broadcast live on radio and televi-sion to ring in the holiday season and brings elation—and shat-tered dreams—to the ticket holders.

In the 1992 draw, ninety-five winning tickets earned a tax-free $2.7 million each. Each ticket costs $270 and is often owned by a syndicate or large group of people.

Compared with other lotteries, the administration costs for *El Gordo* are very low, at 5 percent. Prizes are the largest expense, at 70 percent. The remaining 25 percent goes into the treasury and to various causes. Charitable donations in 1991 included $3.3 million for cancer research and $5.5 million to the Expo World Fair, Olympics, and the Columbus 1492–1992 celebration (see Figure 2.2). Additionally, $5.5 million each was given to the Red Cross and Madrid's Cultural Capital Program (*The Times of London*, December 22, 1992).

Organización Nacional de Ciegos

ONCE is Spain's National Association for the Blind, a group of approximately 34,000 members (*New York Times*, April 2, 1990). Their main fund-raising effort is a weekly numbers lottery, with a second, larger drawing on Fridays. Tickets can be purchased on

Figure 2.2
Allocation to Charities, 1991

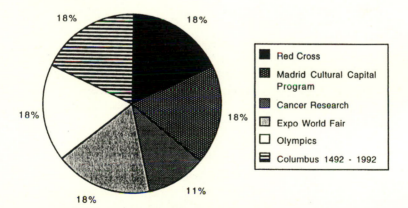

Source: *The Times* (of London), December 22, 1992

any street corner from any of ONCE's 20,000 ticket vendors, many of whom are blind. ONCE's lottery runs in direct competition with the games administered by the government.

Ticket sales in 1989 amounted to $2.5 billion, up from $400,000 in 1982. Of this, half was distributed as prize money. Only 3 percent was given to a foundation for the handicapped. The remaining 47 percent was set aside for the 30,000 salaried employees, 20,000 ticket vendors (who were paid three times the minimum wage), and the 15,000 retired people earning pensions.

A tremendous controversy surrounds the issue of ONCE. Besides operating a lottery, it has investments in construction companies, media organizations, and banks. In fact, it is the fourth or fifth largest investment organization in Spain as well as the second largest advertiser (*The Financial Times of London*, June 4, 1991).

However, it does provide a substantial amount of employment, particularly for the blind. In 1989, for example, ONCE created 1,000 jobs for the blind, awarded 3,000 scholarships, and constructed hospitals, schools, and recreation centers exclusively for blind people. According to Miguel Duràn, "We use our money to create jobs and integrate our group into society" (*New York Times*, April 2, 1990, p. D2).

Gambling in Spain

As stated previously, Spain has a very high gambling population. Per capita expenditures on all forms of gambling amounted to $765 in 1991, putting Spain and the Philippines in a tie for first in per capita expenditures. Of the 39 million people of Spain, 1.7 percent are pathological gamblers, and 5.2 percent are problem gamblers (*The Sunday Telegraph*, May 17, 1992).

The availability of gambling is tremendous. ONCE sells lottery tickets on every street corner, and state lottery tickets are easily purchased in shops. The winning tickets from each game are announced on television. There are also casinos and bingo, but the most popular form of gambling is the slot (or "fruit") machine found in most bars.

While the problem is well known, the Treasury earns $4.2 billion each year from gambling tax revenues. This level of revenue makes it easier to pay so little attention to the 600,000 gambling addicts in their country.

FRANCE

Française des Jeux (FDJ; formerly Franco Loto) enjoyed a 43 percent increase in lottery revenues in 1992 by earning over $5.3 billion. FDJ, the state-owned lottery enterprise, operates two traditional games: Millionaire and *Banco*. Two instant win games, Poker and Blackjack, were introduced in June 1992. France became the first country to operate a real-time lottery system in 1989 when computer equipment was installed in more than 13,500 outlets (*Les Echos,* December 24, 1992).

Another state-owned gambling entity, Pari Mutuel Urbain (PMU), which acts as a bookmaker, has noticed a decline in revenues, while lottery sales have increased. FDJ sees their games as more attractive to young, urban, and female gamblers who are overwhelmed by the complexity of horse racing (*Le Figaro,* January 19, 1993).

FDJ plans to expand by offering gaming products in Germany, Senegal, Italy, and Polynesia, as well as eastern Europe. FDJ chairman Gerard Cole has also recommended selling 21 percent of the state interest in the lottery operation, reducing its share from 72 to 51 percent. This partial privatization would give the Treasury roughly $270 million. Given the Socialist government, many political obstacles stand in the way of this privatization plan (*Les Echos*, September 24, 1992).

RUSSIA

If there are two things Russian people need, they are hope and money. Over the past few years, lotteries have sprung up to satisfy the former need for many and the latter for a few. The main lottery, Million Lotto, is a joint venture with a Greek firm intended to raise funds for athletics. Recently, lotteries for Chernobyl victims and the Goodwill Games have also been introduced.

Million Lotto

Intracom, a Greek firm, invested $20 million in September 1993 to join the financially troubled Olympic Committee to start a lottery. Yellow and blue kiosks have been erected throughout Moscow.

Three 10 ruble tickets are available: a scratch and win game, a pick-six (out of forty-nine) computerized lotto game, and Daily Sports Lotto. Winning numbers are announced on television every Thursday following the local news programs. Average weekly sales have been $78,125 (approximately 35 million rubles). By comparison, California sells that amount in ten minutes. There are 9 million Muscovites to buy lottery tickets, but their average income is only $15 per month. It is quite easy to spend 20 percent of one's wages on lottery tickets (*New York Times*, November 23, 1992).

The odds of winning are slim: For the pick-six game, the odds are 1 in 14 million. The largest jackpot payout has been $38,000. The typical payout is a million rubles, or $2,717—more than 200 times the average Muscovite's salary. Prizes are also awarded to those who correctly select four and five numbers. All winners receive their prizes secretly to prevent theft and jealousy.

The goal of the lottery is to maintain the high quality of representation at Olympic events. Thus, 30 percent of ticket revenues are given to the Olympic Committee. Intracom has rights to 45 percent of earnings, while the Moscow Lottery Organization has a 10 percent interest, and a management consulting firm in Moscow receives 15 percent (*USA Today*, October 5, 1991).

Chernobyl

Dr. Robert Gail, the American bone marrow specialist, went to the then–Soviet Union in order to assist in treating the victims of the 1986 Chernobyl nuclear disaster. With problems unsolved, and coffers running dry, he started up a lottery to generate funds for medical research and treatment.

The tickets, printed in the United States, went on sale in January 1993 and are sold for a dollar (572 rubles, the daily wage for many Russians). Prizes range from $5 to $100,000 (*Newsday*, February 5, 1993).

Goodwill Games

A lottery was also started in 1993 in St. Petersburg to support the 1994 Goodwill Games and the Russian teams. Tickets are priced at 50 rubles (about $0.09), with a top payoff of 2 million rubles (about $3,571) (*New York Times,* February 16, 1993).

Gambling in Russia

Aside from the lottery games available, there are other forms of gambling in Russia. For example, over thirty posh casinos have opened in Moscow for the wealthy Russians.

There are also a number of games of chance played on the streets of Moscow. Although quite popular, most of the game operators rig their games to make it nearly impossible to win.

All forms of gambling are particularly attractive to the one third of the population who live below the poverty line—mostly students, prisoners, and government employees, an income distribution similar to many countries. In the extreme case that is now occurring in Russia, gambling remains one of the few rays of hope for improving one's quality of life.

CHINA

Between its introduction in July 1987 and September 1992, the Chinese Social Welfare Lottery has sold more than $780 million (2.9 billion yuan) worth of tickets. More than $270 million of it has been donated to the Social Welfare Fund. The lottery is part of the Eighth Five-Year Plan, which extends through 1995. There has been steady growth in participation each year. The lottery proceeds have helped in reducing the number of orphans, disabled, and infants who are generally adopted by the state. It also provides relief to disabled people who remain unemployed. Overall, 17,000 projects of varying scope have been at least partially subsidized with lottery revenues. For example, $54 million was provided to assist flood victims in 1991 (*Xinhua General Overseas News Service*, July 14, 1991).

Tickets are available in almost all cities and municipalities in China. The lottery employs approximately 2,000 full-time administrators, in addition to the 20,000 who are engaged in printing, storing, transporting, and selling the tickets. Initially, tickets were lottery draws. However, owing to higher returns, the game has been switching to scratch and win formats known as Instant Tickets in the United States.

Guangzhou

In early 1993, a contract was awarded to a Malaysian firm to set up a lottery in Guangzhou, a city in Guangdong province in southern China. It is the first four-digit game in China. With an initial investment of $16 million, the developers hope to attract many of Guangdong province's 70 million people (*The Financial Times of London*, March 4, 1992).

Sports Lotteries

Several smaller lotteries have been, or will be, set up on a short-term basis to benefit sports. For example, in 1992, a lottery was developed in Shanghai to help finance the inaugural East Asian Games. More than 40 percent of the funds needed for the games are anticipated to come from lotteries throughout China (*Xinhua General Overseas News Service*, June 5, 1992).

Gambling in China

Gambling is quite popular in China. In addition to lotteries, more and more racetracks are being proposed. There have been some severe problems with gambling in the past, however. In 1987, illegal gamblers were arrested at the rate of 1,700 per day. Most of the gambling activities were confined to betting on cards, dice, pool, and various street games. The stakes, though, were approaching $2,700 in many cases. The *China Daily* even reported that a man had to sell his daughter for $220 in order to cover his gambling debts (*Reuters Library Report,* February 8, 1988).

The success of lotteries, therefore, is understandable. Given the population of 1.2 billion, there is tremendous potential for such games. However, the Chinese government is faced with an ideological issue as it confronts the gambling issue. All forms of gambling were banned when the Communist Party took over in 1949. The government maintains that gambling is one of the seven evils—the others being prostitution, slavery, kidnapping, drugs, pornography, and feudal superstition. For Malaysian Chinese, many of whom are Muslim, gambling is also forbidden by religion. This is a serious issue in Malaysia, where gambling is growing very quickly. In fact, horse racing and lottery operations are regarded as "Blue Chips" in their stock market, accounting for 10 percent of all capital listed on the market (*South China Morning Post,* February 9, 1993).

IRELAND

Ireland's lottery system was established in 1986 and has paid out over $253 million of its $722 million revenues to a variety of charities including sports, cultural, youth, health, and social welfare organizations. Approximately half the revenues have been awarded as prizes; the typical payout is in the neighborhood of $2 million (*Press Association Newsfile,* December 24, 1992).

There are two games available: a pick-six lotto, which is responsible for 65.1 percent of the revenues; and an instant game, which makes up the remaining 34.9 percent. Nearly 60 percent of adults play the games regularly. (Very few people in Northern Ireland play lottery games, however.) Tickets are sold through agents who receive 6.3 percent of revenue. Another 10 percent is held for administration costs (*Irish Times,* February 26, 1993).

As in most countries, lower-class citizens actively participate in lottery games. For example, 59 percent of unemployed persons play regularly, spending an average of nearly $2 per week, 4 percent above the national average. Also, in spite of a worsening economy, participation in the lottery games actually rose 6 percent in 1992.

Many people are concerned about the effect lottery games has had on charitable donations. While nearly 90 percent of Ireland's 3.5 million people donate at least once a month, 25 percent of the more popular charitable organizations claim a decline in giving since the introduction of a national lottery (*Press Association Newsfile*, February 3, 1993). The favored charities include the St. Vincent de Paul Society, which helps the poor; cancer research organizations; and Third World assistance programs.

GREAT BRITAIN

The issue of lotteries in Great Britain has been faced differently than in other countries since lottery games will not be available until August 1994. Owing to the popularity of lotteries throughout Europe and the United States, Britons have been calling for games of their own for many years. After overcoming political hurdles, officials studied lottery operations throughout the past two years to develop their own games.

Lottery officials are hoping for annual revenues of $2 billion. This represents per capita spending of $18 (*Daily Telegraph*, January 25, 1993). Like Ireland, there will be two games available: a lotto game played through computerized terminals in shops all over Britain and an instant scratch and win game. For the lotto game, weekly jackpot payouts of $1.5 million are expected. Many smaller prizes will also be awarded. Tickets will cost £1.

Of the revenues, 30 percent will be paid out in prizes, 15 percent will be held for administration fees, and 30 percent will be awarded to charities. The remainder of the revenues will go to the Treasury (see Figure 2.3). The charitable awards will go primarily to the arts, sports, heritage projects, the Millennium Fund (cultural

Figure 2.3
Revenue Distribution of British Lottery

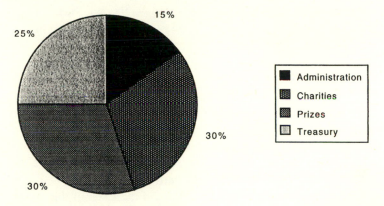

Source: *The Economist,* April 17, 1992

venue restoration), and a variety of other social causes (*Chicago Tribune,* December 23, 1992).

The biggest issue surrounding the proposed lottery is how much it will be taxed. The Heritage Committee, which oversees the lottery, is hoping for a tax rate of less than 10 percent, preferably 5 percent. The Treasury, however, wants 20 percent.

Gambling in Britain

A national lottery is certainly not the advent of gambling in Britain. Already, 70 percent of Britons gamble, spending $7 per capita per week. The most popular form of gambling is soccer betting pools with 16 million customers and worth about $544 million to the Treasury last year. Pool operators fear the loss of up to 30 percent of their business with the introduction of a lottery, forcing them to cut their workforce from 6,500 to 3,000 (*The Observer,* December 8, 1992).

While the British do not yet have their own lottery games, those of other countries have been quite popular. Many people have bought Irish tickets, and last year millions of German lottery tickets were confiscated en route to Britain. This issue has given strength to the argument that Britain needs its own lottery. Obviously, if the people are going to play the games, their country wants the revenue from them.

Not Everyone Wants a Lottery

Despite the overwhelming demand for a lottery, many objections have been raised regarding its introduction. Most of the registered objections are on moral grounds or are in disagreement with the anticipated charities. Also, many fear a detrimental effect on voluntary donations to British charities.

The moral objections mainly surround the issue of the games' attractiveness to lower-class citizens. People fear that the poor will be gambling their dreams away. Protesters suggest this situation is furthered because wealthier people tend to utilize the cultural opportunities lottery revenues provide more than lower-class citizens. Others are concerned about the lottery's age requirement: Players have to be only sixteen.

Naturally, there are concerns about advancing gambling addiction. Lottery officials have tried to dispel such worries, noting that the odds of winning deter most serious gamblers. Indeed, the projected odds of winning the lotto game are 1 in 9 million, and 1 in 6 for the instant games.

Still others are disappointed with the selection of charities for lottery proceeds. Particularly controversial are donations for sports, which not everyone enjoys, and the Millennium Fund, which many see as unnecessary and wasteful. Given high rates of unemployment and the high level of need of most charitable organizations, these people see more equitable projects for the lottery revenues. Preferred targets include medical research and care for the elderly and children.

The fear that voluntary donations will decrease has been triggered largely by the sharp decline of giving in Ireland after the introduction of a national lottery. A British consulting firm supports this concern, suggesting British fund-raisers could see a 7 to 14 percent decline in donations (*The Observer,* July 19, 1992).

A Lottery to Aid the Unemployed

In 1993, a lottery was established in Pembrokeshire, West Wales, to provide financial assistance to the area. In many parts of this region, unemployment has reached 30 percent. The organization, made up of one manager and four assistants, sells 25,000 tickets per week, one of which comes with a $2,000 prize. It is anticipated that over $670,000 will be raised each year. Area businesses needing assistance, and wanting to protect jobs, can apply for funding (*Press Association Newsfile,* March 30, 1993).

OTHER COUNTRIES

Many smaller countries also administer lotteries to raise money for their Treasury or a specific cause. A few examples have been selected based on their unique issues.

Albania

Until 1993, Albania was the only European holdout, besides Britain, from the lottery craze. Planning their first Olympic appearance since 1972, Albania was seriously in need of funding for the 1992 Summer Olympic team. To support this venture, a lottery was started. It continues to operate to support Olympic training facilities.

The instant win, scratch-off tickets are available at Albania's twenty-seven savings banks for about $0.50. Prizes range from $10 to $5,000, which is twice the average annual salary in Albania (*Wall Street Journal,* March 9, 1992).

In lieu of cash, winners may redeem their tickets for Western consumer goods. This propensity for American goods doesn't stop there. The Albanian Finance Ministry prefers to sell the tickets for dollars or drachma rather than their unstable lek. Additionally, each ticket bears the American flag—symbolic of Albanian people's distrust of their own government.

Poland

Poland has been saturated with lottery games, both nationally and privately run. *Totolotek*, the most popular game, is run by the state enterprise Totalizator Sportowy. Over 550 terminals have been installed in Warsaw and Katowice and are radio connected. Approximately 1.5 million play *Totolotek* regularly. An instant win game called *Rekord* was also released in 1992 (*Warsaw Voice*, January 19, 1992).

Indonesia

The state-sponsored lottery in Indonesia takes in over $9 million every week, awarding prizes as high as $500,000. However, the lottery is extremely controversial. A high percentage of Indonesians are practicing Muslims. Muslim teaching strictly prohibits any form of gambling. This conflict has led to many protests of the lottery, particularly by students. Some charities that have received funds from lottery revenues have gone so far as to return the money, claiming it is "tainted" (*The Economist,* December 21, 1991).

COMMON ISSUES FACING LOTTERY OPERATORS

In examining the various lottery setups throughout the world, there are two major sets of issues or questions that every lottery faces: First, should the state (government) set up a lottery? This is the "start-up" question. Second, once it has been decided to set up a lottery, how should the lottery be operated? This is the "operational" question. The type of specific issues that these questions lend themselves to will be delineated below and will be the focus of the rest of this chapter.

Start-up Issues

The start-up issues are a combination of economic and political justifications that are used both for and against the establishment of a government(state)-operated lottery. The economic debate over a lottery is centered around two questions:

1. How much new revenue will the lottery be able to provide the state? The answer to this question will depend greatly on what games and type of gambling will be introduced.
2. Will this funding be consistent—can interest in lottery games be maintained? The answers to this question will have a marked impact on the debate surrounding the next set of political questions. They will be the focus of Chapters 4 and 5.

The political questions surrounding the establishment of a lottery can be divided into two categories:

1. Should the state be involved in the gambling industry? In answering this question, there are, of course, religious and other ethical arguments that will be made. Even supporters of a lottery will generally concede that a lottery is a necessary evil but one that can and should be "tolerated." Chapter 3 discusses the ethical arguments that are used to build tolerance for a lottery.
2. If the answer to the preceding question is affirmative, then public policy makers are faced with the problem of deciding for what purposes lottery funding should be used. In most European lotteries, lottery proceeds are used to fund charitable works (e.g., Spain, Ireland), whereas in the United States, we will see these funds go directly into the general revenue fund. The question of who gets lottery funding is one that will have a profound impact on the next set of operational issues.

Operational Issues

The operational issues are ultimately tied to the economic and political issues that were just discussed. There is certainly an "evolutionary" aspect to the operation of a lottery and gambling questions, which we saw as we examined the various lottery operations throughout the world. The three evolutionary stages that a lottery appears to undergo are (1) takeoff, (2) diversification, and (3) privatization. There will be a brief discussion of these stages now, but a more detailed discussion of these phenomena appears in Chapters 4, 5, 6, and 7.

The takeoff stage that lottery commissions face is simply the choice of game(s) to spark the interest of the public in playing lottery games. In Spain, the initial lottery offerings were "sweepstakes" games, while in Great Britain the lottery commission will begin its lottery operations with lotto and scratch games. This choice of beginning games will, as we will see, have a profound effect on how lottery officials can introduce other games or forms of gambling at a later period.

The diversification stage of lottery development is one where lottery officials must decide what combination of games will "maximize" revenue without alienating antigambling groups. The key issue that lottery officials face during this phase of operations could be termed the *cannibalization effect* when new games are introduced. For example, the sales of Great Britain's lotto games might dramatically decrease after lottery officials introduce various "scratch" games. In other words, total revenue from lottery operations is not nearly as high as lottery officials predicted because the total lottery market was much smaller than expected.

In the final stage of lottery operations, public policy officials are faced with the issue of expanding state-sponsored lottery operations in order to make them more "efficient." In China and Russia, lottery games were being operated by private owners who had the equipment and know-how to operate large lottery operations. In France, there is a similar call to privatize lottery operations. But this efficiency question could also lead public policy officials to expand possible gambling activities beyond merely sponsoring lotteries. These additional forms of gambling—such as video poker machines, keno, and casino gambling—once again force public officials to face the question, Is it appropriate for government to be operating these forms of gambling, or are these forms of gambling better suited for private operation? Thus, government search for additional revenue ironically often ends up with the state ending its direct operation of gambling activities.

But before the question of privatizing gambling activities can be analyzed, there needs to be an examination of why the public tolerates government activity in the gambling industry in the first place, the focus of Chapter 3.

Chapter 3

The Triumph of the "Ethics of Tolerance": The Evolution of Lotteries in the Public Policy Process

The two preceding chapters have chronicled the existence of the lottery in the United States and in other countries of the world. The fact that lotteries and other forms of gambling are sponsored in so many parts of the world is very revealing. But what is even more intriguing is the fact that in almost every instance the institution of a lottery or any other kind of state-sponsored gambling has been surrounded by controversy. Invariably, the controversy that public policy makers face involves a conflict between those who maintain that the goal of public policy should be to maintain the "societal good" versus those who advocate the supremacy of the "rights of the individual."

Those who advocate the institution of a state lottery or other forms of gambling will appeal to a very different ethical argument. They will argue that people are natural gamblers and will gamble whether or not the government allows gambling. So since people are going to gamble, shouldn't government legalize gambling as long as it uses these gambling proceeds for a good purpose? After all, government cannot legislate morality.

Meanwhile, those who oppose the adoption of lotteries or other types of state-sponsored gambling usually invoke the argument that lotteries and gambling prey on the poor or those who become addicted to gambling. Therefore, it is in the best interest of society that lotteries and gambling be outlawed. They would maintain that society cannot permit any activity that uses the addiction of some segment even if the rest of society might derive benefit.

In the United States, this conflict between the societal good and the rights of the individual has been the focus of the ethical controversy surrounding numerous U.S. public policy debates throughout its history. Debates over controversial issues such as slavery, taxation, and states' rights were constantly appealing to either of these ethical schools in making their cases either pro or con. It is still the basis for debating the ethical merits of public policy issues, ranging from environmental issues to gun control. Hence, throughout U.S. history, public policy makers have had to constantly balance this conflict between the common good versus the right of the individual to choose freely. It has resulted in what will be referred to as the "ethics of sacrifice" and the "ethics of tolerance."

The rest of this chapter will be used to examine these two schools of ethical argumentation in the United States and elsewhere. First, each ethic will be described in detail—especially how the ethic is used by public policy makers to establish their policy positions. Next, the lottery and gambling issue will be contrasted with the cigarette-smoking issue to see how each ethic is employed. Finally, there will be a brief discussion on which of these ethics seems to be prevailing in the U.S. public policy forum currently.

ETHICS OF SACRIFICE

When sacrifice is used as a moral concept to advance the merits of a particular public policy issue, public policy makers must be able to persuade the public that it must give up some benefit or right in order to achieve a noble goal or end. While it can easily be invoked by religious leaders, it can also be employed by political leaders in times of great national crisis, especially in times of popular wars such as World War I and World War II. In terms of traditional ethical or moral categories, the ethics of sacrifice is teleological; that is, it is goal or end oriented. The goal is the good of society, and the goodness of any action is measured by what it contributes to maintaining the good of society.

In terms of public policy, the "good end" is a harmonious society. Traditionally, this ethic has been invoked by those who want to maintain social structure that they deem as desirable and that should be maintained at any cost. Witness the concern of public policy makers over maintaining "family values." While some might associate this type of ethical reasoning with conservative policy makers, it actually has been used by both conservative and liberal thinkers to justify their stance on major public policy issues. Liberal politicians such as John F. Kennedy certainly invoked the ethics of sacrifice with his famous phrase: "Ask not what your country can do for you; ask what you can do for your country!" In essence, those who utilize the ethics of sacrifice are asking the public to sublimate what is good for the individual for the good of all.

An interesting example of a public policy issue in which supporters invoked the ethics of sacrifice was Prohibition. Supporters of this total ban on alcohol consumption argued that the abuse of alcohol was a factor that led to the disintegration of many families throughout the United States. So in order to preserve the sanctity of the family, the right of a person to drink alcohol had to be sacrificed. Society could no longer condone the waste of human life that could be attributed to alcohol. In the eyes of prohibitionists, the good that was achieved through the establishment of Prohibition more than outweighed the right of an individual to drink alcohol. However, it soon became apparent that the majority of the public were quite unwilling to make the sacrifice of avoiding the use of alcoholic beverages. Prohibition was repealed, and this experiment of enforced sacrificial morality was abandoned.

At its most extreme, those who invoke the ethics of sacrifice can be accused of employing the motto "The ends justify the means." The individual's ability to decide what is best for himself or herself needs to be subservient to the needs of the state. The good of the state overrides the rights and needs of the individual. This ethic is certainly the one under which the military and religious orders operate. However, when it is applied to a society with many diverse parts, it can have disastrous consequences. One only need recall the Communist experience throughout the past five decades. Yet it is an ethic that calls forth what some would maintain is the noblest of human characteristics: the ability to give of oneself even if that giving is detrimental to that individual.

ETHICS OF TOLERANCE

One of the earliest virtues that every American schoolchild is taught is tolerance. To escape religious persecution in England, the Quakers settled in Pennsylvania and are celebrated in American history texts because they permitted everyone to practice their religious beliefs. In founding Maryland, Lord Baltimore also established freedom of religion, especially for persecuted English Catholics, although this religious tolerance would be tested frequently throughout the colonial period. The Pilgrims who settled Massachusetts were also trying to escape religious persecution; however, tolerance was not a Puritan virtue, as Roger Williams quickly found out when he was forced to flee Massachusetts to establish Rhode Island. While there have been difficulties throughout U.S. history, in comparison with most societies, tolerance for different religions as well as different nationalities has been one of the hallmarks of American society.

Tolerance entails that no person has to sacrifice his or her basic freedoms in order to achieve some goal of public welfare. Society cannot tolerate the abandonment of any individual even if society must incur a heavy cost to save that individual from activities that are harmful to that individual. It also entails that American society has to tolerate the right of the individual to perform actions that might very well be destructive to that society as long as that right to perform those activities is guaranteed by law. In traditional ethical thought, the ethics of tolerance would fall into the deontological mode of thinking; that is, the means that a person uses to achieve a goal are as important as the goal itself.

A recent example of where the ethics of tolerance has so far prevailed in the public policy forum is the gun control issue. Opponents of gun controls have used the ethics of tolerance as the basis of their moral public policy argument. They maintain that the right to bear arms has to be tolerated even if the majority of the nation wishes to put some limits on this right. Society has to tolerate the possible improper use of guns in order to uphold the rights of a minority who wish to have no limits on their ability to own guns.

The ethics of tolerance is based on a noble American value and experiment—never to view a citizen as a means to achieve an end. Government exists to protect the individual's rights and must not coerce an individual to relinquish a right even for a good purpose. It is a value that in many ways is a necessity in a country of immigrants. Immigrants have to be tolerated and protected in order to promote diversity in a society. But like most values, this ethic also has its downside. At its worst, the ethics of tolerance can promote a rather narrow, selfish focus on the individual with little regard for how individuals need to relate to one another in order to live in a society. For this glorification of the individual makes it quite difficult for society to be able to challenge the individual to make the sacrifices that are necessary so that everyone in that society can live together harmoniously.

GAMBLING AND SMOKING: A SURVEY OF THE PAST THIRTY YEARS (1964–1994)

In 1964, cigarette smoking was an activity that was tolerated both by public policy makers and by the public at large as a harmless, perhaps slightly unhealthy, pastime. For public policy makers, cigarette smoking was viewed as a source of income that could be justified by leveling excise taxes known as "sin" taxes. Cigarette smokers considered smoking a right to which they were entitled in order to deal with the various stresses of life. If they were harming anyone, it was only themselves. Antismoking forces insisted that cigarette smoking ought to be discouraged if not outlawed since it was in society's best social interest. However, the economic benefits from cigarette production as well as the rights of the cigarette smokers triumphed over the "societal good" argument.

Meanwhile, in 1964, gambling was roundly condemned by most segments of U.S. society. Casino gambling was confined to

Nevada, and horse and dog racing were tolerated because they were "sporting" events that were made possible by betting on the various races. New Hampshire had just become the first state to approve a lottery in a very controversial election. Prior to this newly legalized state-sponsored lottery, only charitable institutions such as churches, fire companies, and the like, were permitted to run bingo games—fifty-fifty chances—in order to provide revenue for good causes. But in general, government at all levels— bowing to public sentiment, discouraged gambling. It was considered an activity that was not tolerable, and therefore the right to gamble was easily sacrificed.

Yet in less than thirty years these two activities have experienced an almost complete role reversal in their places in the public policy process. A majority of the U.S. population view cigarette smokers as pariahs who are to be banished from offices and most public places, whereas gambling is now considered a legitimate form of entertainment in most sections of the United States with the exception of the Bible Belt South.

The rest of this chapter will explain just how these issues have evolved so differently over the course of the past thirty years. First, there will be a brief review of the history of the cigarette industry in this country. Next, an explanation of how these issues have evolved will be made using the frameworks of the ethics of sacrifice and the ethics of tolerance. Finally, there will be a commentary on how these frameworks are being utilized in developing public policy positions today.

Cigarettes and Public Policy Makers:
A Historical Perspective

Government regulation of the cigarette industry has always involved a curious blend of economic and moral rationales. In fact, the cigarette industry, like the lottery, has gone through three phases of regulation. Figures 3.1, 3.2, and 3.3 illustrate the three waves of cigarette regulation in this country.

Figure 3.1
First Wave: The Structure of the Industry, 1911–1964

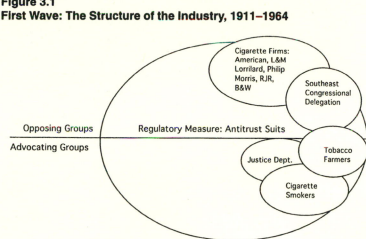

Figure 3.2
Second Wave: The Health of the Smoker, 1964–1985

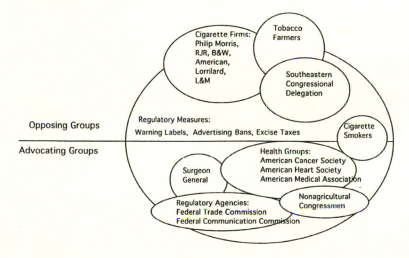

Figure 3.3
The Third Wave: The Rights of the Nonsmoker, 1985–present

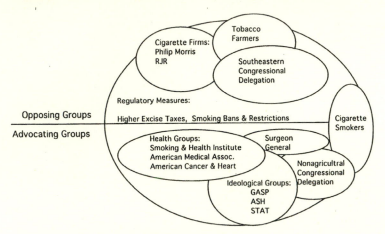

The first wave of regulation (1911–1964) was occasioned by the oligopolistic structure of the industry. Antitrust activity was the chief weapon of regulators in order to ensure that cigarette smokers could obtain their cigarettes at a "fair" price. Cigarette excise taxes, at both the federal and state levels of government, were imposed to penalize those who engage in this slightly unsavory activity and to serve as a source of needed revenue. There was no question about an individual's right to smoke; rather, the point of controversy was the smoker's access to a cigarette at an affordable price and whether it was fair to tax cigarettes. Society had to tolerate smoking even if it appeared that it was not an activity that benefited the individual or society at large.

The second wave of regulation (1964–1985) was ignited by the surgeon general's report, which linked cigarette smoking and cancer. It now became the goal of public policy makers to discourage cigarette smoking. To respond to this goal, legislators at the federal level forced cigarette makers to put warning labels on cigarette packages and banned cigarette advertising on radio and TV. Excise taxes were raised at all levels of government not only to discourage cigarette use but also to raise more revenue for government coffers. However, the right of an individual to smoke cigarettes was never questioned. Policy makers were always reminded of this right whenever they were about to enact legislation that affected cigarette smokers.

Meanwhile, the antismoking forces began to agitate for banning all cigarette smoking. Besides the health issue, the other major argument that they employed was an economic one, namely, that cigarette smoking was extremely costly to society in terms of premature deaths as well as time lost in the workplace. Hence, antismoking groups maintained that the right to smoke could no longer be tolerated because of economic *and* health reasons. However, the cigarette industry countered this economic argument of the antismoking groups by pointing out the enormous amount of revenue that cigarettes generated both for retailers and for tobacco farmers and of course for government in the form of excise taxes. In the end, the cigarette industry was able to avoid overwhelming government interference in the industry through its use of the ethics of tolerance and its ability to counter some of the antismoking groups' economic arguments.

The third wave of regulation (1985–present) was triggered by another surgeon general report on "passive smoking" or "secondhand smoke." This report concluded that cigarette smoke was causing higher-than-normal cancer rates even for non–cigarette smokers if they were living or working with cigarette smokers. With the issuance of this report, the issue of the rights of the nonsmoker came into the public policy arena. Immediately, laws were passed that barred cigarette smoking from public areas and offices in order to protect the nonsmoker from the dangers of even secondhand cigarette smoke. Another factor that led to this lack of tolerance of cigarette smoking was the decreasing economic importance of the cigarette industry itself. Since 1983, cigarette sales had been declining continuously, and so the industry's economic contribution no longer covered the health costs of cigarette smokers.

Antismoking groups now had both a rights argument and an economic argument on their side. The rights of the smokers

became secondary to those of the nonsmoker when it was shown
that cigarette smoking affected not only the smokers but also the
nonsmokers who also had to breathe the smoke-filled air. In this
third wave of regulation, the antismoking forces were able to use
arguments that employed both the ethics of sacrifice and the ethics
of tolerance.

Comparing the Evolution of the Lottery and Smoking Issues

In comparing the evolution of these two controversial public
policy issues—namely, smoking and gambling—it would be
instructive to summarize the roles that the ethics of sacrifice and
the ethics of tolerance have played in determining the past and present status of these issues.

Tables 3.1 and 3.2 catalog for each of these public policy issues
the primary type of ethical argument that both advocates (those
who wish to legalize lotteries, etc. or to limit government involvement in the cigarette industry) and opponents (of gambling or cigarette smoking) used in establishing their positions during the
various waves of public policy activity.

Table 3.1
The Evolution of Smoking and Ethical Argumentation

Evolution of Smoking	Advocates	Opponents
First wave	Ethics of tolerance	Ethics of sacrifice
Second wave	Ethics of tolerance	Ethics of sacrifice
Third wave	Ethics of tolerance	Ethics of tolerance
		Ethics of sacrifice

Table 3.2
The Evolution of Lotteries (Gambling) and Ethical Argumentation

Evolution of Lotteries	Advocates	Opponents
First wave	Ethics of tolerance	Ethics of sacrifice
Second wave	Ethics of tolerance	Ethics of sacrifice
Third wave	Ethics of tolerance	Ethics of sacrifice

In viewing these tables, one is struck by these three observations: First, advocates of either legalizing lotteries (or other types of gambling activities) or reducing government involvement in the cigarette industry invariably employ the ethics of tolerance as their primary moral argument when approaching the public policy arena. Their argument for both issues is simply that society must tolerate these activities since individuals should have the right to engage in them as long as they are not harming anyone else. These advocates also attempt to counter the ethics of sacrifice argument by noting the potential economic contributions of these "sin industries." While they acknowledge that activities might be harmful to some individuals, the state or charities ought to be able to profit from these activities since most smokers or gamblers will continue to smoke or gamble whether or not the state permits these activities. So why shouldn't the state or a charity use the profit from them for a good cause?

Meanwhile, opponents of these two "sinful" activities have generally employed the ethics of sacrifice as their primary ethical resource in their fights against these vices. They would argue that any benefits that accrue to society by allowing these activities in no way justifies them. Society must protect itself from activities that bring great harm on various segments of society. The harm done to society at large more than outweighs the harm done by violating an individual's right to engage in these activities. Therefore, government ought to sacrifice lotteries (all other types of gambling) and the rights of cigarette smokers for society's overall good.

But perhaps the most interesting item from these tables occurs in the row for the third wave of each table. These results indicate that a remarkable change has taken place in the public policy process, namely, the triumph of the ethics of tolerance. In Table 3.1, one is immediately struck that the ethics of tolerance is now being used by the opponents of the cigarette industry to make their case against the cigarette industry. Since the primary force behind the third wave of regulation of the cigarette industry has been the passive smoking issue, opponents of the industry are now able to employ the following argument: Cigarette smokers no longer have the right to smoke because it has been proven that nonsmokers are negatively affected by cigarette smoke. In other words, the right to smoke can no longer be tolerated since it interferes with the rights of nonsmokers to live in a smoke-free environment.

Meanwhile, Table 3.2 also confirms another triumph for the ethics of tolerance. The recent surge in establishing state lotteries as well as other forms of state-sponsored gambling indicates that public policy makers sense that the majority of their constituencies are in agreement with the tenets of the ethics of tolerance in regard to the gambling issue. Indeed, when it comes to the lottery and gambling issue, it appears that the public is *not* willing to sacrifice the right to gamble nor the income that comes from state-sponsored gambling.

Implications of the Triumph of the Ethics of Tolerance

In trying to understand why two public policy issues such as lotteries (gambling) and smoking have evolved so differently over the past thirty years, the conclusion reached was that there has been a change in the basic ethic that motivates public policy makers. It represents the triumph of the rights of individuals (ethics of tolerance) over the good of a society (ethics of sacrifice). With the triumph of the ethics of tolerance, it appears that the new categorical imperative that public policy makers operate under is: "You have the right to perform any action as long as that action does not interfere with the rights of others."

This triumph of the ethics of tolerance does not preclude the ethics of sacrifice from playing a significant role in the current public policy process nor guarantee that the ethics of sacrifice might not triumph again in the future. But this triumph of the ethics of tolerance does indicate that at least for the foreseeable future most public policy issues will be settled in favor of those who can employ the arguments that can be generated from the ethics of tolerance. Perhaps the following examples of current public policy issues will clarify further this triumph of the ethics of tolerance. One example of where the ethics of tolerance will play a vital role in deciding the outcome of a controversial public policy issue is health care. It certainly appears that the health care plan that will be chosen will have to ensure that the patient will have the right to choose a physician and that medical care is provided at a reasonable cost. The American public does not appear willing to tolerate a lack of choice in choosing its doctors nor willing to tolerate the high cost of medical care. It will also be interesting to observe whether public policy makers can persuade the public to tolerate the position that everyone has the right to access to health care, especially if this right to universal medical care might prohibit the right of the individual to choose the type of medical care he or she wants.

Another recent example of the triumph of the ethics of tolerance over the ethics of sacrifice was a successful suit that overturned a service requirement mandated by the Bethlehem, Pennsylvania, school district in order for students to graduate from high school. When the board of the school district demanded that its high school graduates be required to be involved in sixty hours of service work for the community, it used as its rationale a quote from Robert Vaux, the founder of the Pennsylvania public school system: "Education constitutes the moral strength and beauty of every state and forms the only sure basis upon which a good society can rest." Vaux also stated that the mission of the public school was to ensure "the universal diffusion of intelligence and the cultivation of good morals in young people." However, the court seemed to put aside the good purpose of the public school system in ruling that this requirement "subjected students to involuntary servitude and unconstitutionally forces them to submit to a government-approved belief in altruism" (*Philadelphia Inquirer*, December 29, 1993, p. A11). It certainly appears that the court in its ruling used the ethics of tolerance over any consideration of the common good. The right of the individual had to be tolerated even if the primary purpose of education is to ensure that an individual can learn to contribute to society.

With this discussion of the ethics of sacrifice and the ethics of tolerance, the analysis of the various public policy processes that have contributed to the current lotteries and gambling situation in the United States is completed. It is now time to turn to examine the business policies that the various directors of lotteries employ in operating their lotteries. As these business policies of the various lotteries are examined, it should become clear to the reader that these two social processes (i.e., business and public policies) are interrelated. Obviously, public policy makers had to give their approval before the operations of a lottery (or any other form of gambling) could begin. Hence, one of the goals of lottery operators is to maintain this approval by being quite responsive to public policy makers' wishes in conducting their lotteries. At the same time, however, it will also become readily apparent that public policy makers will need to respond to the need of lottery directors to develop an overall business strategy in operating their state-sponsored gambling ventures if these lotteries are going to be able to meet the revenue needs for the various designated good causes. This intertwining of the business and public processes, which characterizes the current state of gambling in the United States, ought to provide the reader with some interesting insights as to how these two processes might work in other industries that are currently under state control but could soon become privatized.

PART II

THE STRATEGIC MANAGEMENT OF LOTTERIES

Chapter 4

Lottery Games and the Various Strategies for Conducting Lotteries

The thesis of the preceding chapters argued that lotteries (gambling in general) are a form of entertainment that American society has tolerated in varying degrees throughout its history. The level of that toleration varies according to the need of government for revenue versus a society's need to regulate activity that it deems as unhealthy but not necessarily evil if that activity can be used to raise funds for good causes. Hence, a lottery commissioner must always take these two factors into account as he or she is formulating a strategy by which he or she hopes to run this lottery.

One helpful way of defining the term *strategy* is to use its Greek origins as the "art of the general." While the militaristic connotations of this definition frighten many individuals, it does provide a very useful analogy for those who operate any organization, particularly a lottery. A general cannot make a strategy for defending or attacking unless he or she is ready to cover all the flanks. Similarly, a lottery director is faced with many issues that can expose the director to attacks from many sides. A lottery commissioner has to be able to satisfy a variety of governmental interests such as the legislature and the executive branch as well as a host of interested social groups who oppose gambling ranging from church groups to Gamblers Anonymous.

But besides taking into account the interests of various constituencies, a lottery commissioner must carefully determine the type of business he or she is engaged in. Just who are the competitors for the dollars that bettors spend on the lottery? Most commentators on lotteries as well as the lottery commissioners themselves agree that the lottery is a form of entertainment. Like all other forms of entertainment, it provides its users with an outlet for escape or a way to fulfill a dream. Since different bettors have different dreams, a lottery needs to provide different outlets for different dreams. Variety is the spice of life, and this truism is especially applicable to businesses that are trying to provide for those who have a need to change their lives. Because a lottery is a form of entertainment and escape, in formulating and implementing a strategic plan for a state lottery, a lottery commissioner needs to develop a variety of games for his or her customers. Hence, the vast majority of lotteries have "diversified" into all three games (daily numbers, instant games, lotto). Out of the thirty-eight states that sponsor lotteries, only three do not sponsor all three games. The only game that these three states do not offer is the daily number, while all of the states offer a lotto game and instant games. As part of state-sponsored gambling activity, states are also introducing casino gambling and video games (mostly poker games).

But even though all lotteries have used an overall diversification strategy, it is striking to observe how certain games predominate the operations of most lotteries. If one examines Table 4.1, it becomes readily apparent that most lotteries are actually using a "niche" strategy, that is, focusing on one type of lottery game while operating the other types of games.

Why has this niche strategy for operating a lottery become so common? It has a great deal to do with the primary reason why a state sanctions a lottery; that is, the primary goal of a lottery is to be a *consistent* source of revenue for state government, thereby making the lottery a tolerable enterprise. A successful lottery is one that is consistent in two ways:

1. It is able to provide additional revenue for states when legislatures and governors are in search of additional revenue sources in order to bal-

Table 4.1
Lottery Niches In Various States

Lotto Games account for at least 50 percent of all lottery revenue

Arizona	Colorado	Washington
Florida	Illinois	New Hampshire
Vermont	Maine	California

Daily number Games account for at least 50 percent of all lottery revenue

District of Columbia	New Jersey	Maryland
Pennsylvania	Delaware	New York

Instant Games account for at least 50 percent of all lottery revenue

Massachusetts	Wisconsin	Minnesota
Iowa	West Virginia	Kansas
Ohio	Texas	

Video Games account for at least 50 percent of lottery revenue

Atlantic(Canadian)	South Dakota

ance a state's budget. In the foreseeable future, state governments will be faced with an ever-increasing need to supplement their revenue needs with different sources of revenue rather than raising traditional sources of revenue such as sales, income, and property taxes. One measure of a successful lottery will be its ability to provide a state additional revenue in time of need; hence, the game must be able to provide additional revenues when they are needed. To ascertain whether a game is capable of future growth, we will need to establish where a game is on its product life cycle and whether this cycle can be "renewed."

2. A second criterion for a consistent lottery game involves the concept of "cannibalizing" existing games. While the sales of a new game might increase rapidly, if it merely "steals" customers from existing games, then it provides no new lottery revenue. A more positive way of looking at this issue is to ask the question: Upon which game can a lottery commissioner build future lottery games or institute different forms of gambling without affecting existing lottery sales? This criterion will be examined in Chapter 5.

Hence, in evaluating the strategy that a state employs for operating its lottery, two criteria need to be employed. A lottery can be judged to be successful (1) if it is one that is capable of providing growth in sales and (2) if it can introduce new games or other forms of gambling without cannibalizing the sales of existing lottery games. This chapter will examine the first of these criteria— that is, Is there a lottery strategy capable of sustained long-term growth? This growth criterion will be studied in three parts. In the first part, the various strategic options for operating a lottery will be classified. Then the concept of a product life cycle will be applied to the various lottery games. Finally, an evaluation of existing strategies will be made and the future prospects for these strategies will be examined.

CLASSIFYING LOTTERY STRATEGIES

It has already been pointed out that lottery commissioners seem to be employing a niche strategy in operating their lotteries. In order to identify and evaluate these niche strategies, an analogy will be used to classify these niches that corresponds with the strategies that the general manager of a professional baseball team must develop in order to build a consistently successful team. The reason why general managers develop different strategies in building their teams is to take advantage of the type of ballpark in which a team plays its home games. General managers are simply building their teams to correspond to their environments, and the same is true in establishing a strategy for operating a lottery: Develop the game that takes advantage of the demographics of the state.

Strategy 1: Instant Games—Playing for a Series of One-Run Innings

Some general managers need to build a team that allows them to take advantage of a ballpark that rewards speed and hence doesn't reward a team trying to play for a big inning. Since home runs will be hard to hit, the offense must be built around the notion of playing for many one-run innings. To get these one-run innings, the general manager must provide the team with the ability to get a lot of "single hitters" and then have a speedy team that can take advantage of the abundance of runners who can score runs. Lotteries that focus on instant games for the bulk of their revenue are using the "big ballpark" strategy (see Table 4.2). The lottery commissioner must provide a

Table 4.2
States Using Instant Games as the Focus of Their Lotteries, 1992

State	Lotto	Daily Number	Instant	Total
Massachusetts	1.05 (18.8)	1.49 (24.3)	3.84 (56.8)	6.13
Ohio	1.09 (33.1)	.92 (29.0)	1.16 (37.9)	3.17
Wisconsin	.37 (15.6)	.33 (13.9)	1.66 (70.3)	2.36

Source: Massachusetts Lottery Commission

continual stream of instant games. He or she also must move quickly to market different games for different seasons as well as appeal to different customers. While no one instant game will be the source of an enormous amount of revenue, if enough successful ones are continually introduced, the strategy can be termed a success.

Table 4.2 presents the breakdown of lottery proceeds from those states that have used instant games as the primary focus of their lottery efforts. The table shows the per capita spent per week (1992 figures) on each game, and the figure in parentheses shows the percentage of sales of the total lottery proceeds.

Strategy 2: Lotto Games—Playing for the "Big Inning"

In emphasizing the lotto game as the source of strategic focus, a lottery commissioner is emulating the general manager of a baseball team whose offensive strategy is to play for the big inning— that is, have a few single hitters who are on base when the home run hitters come to bat. It is basically a sit-back-in-your-seat strategy insofar as the team is dependent on the home run hitters to connect every once in a while so that sufficient offense is produced. Lotto games operate in a very similar fashion. Successful lotto games have to be able to generate very large jackpots in order to generate interest in the game. In other words, the home run for a lotto game is its ability to generate a huge jackpot. It doesn't happen every week, but hopefully it occurs often enough so that it keeps the players' interest alive and attracts other players, resulting in even larger jackpots.

Table 4.3 presents the breakdown of lottery proceeds from those states that have used lotto games as the primary focus of their lottery efforts. The table shows the per capita spent per week (1992 figures) on each game, and the figure in parentheses shows the percentage of sales of the total lottery proceeds.

Table 4.3
States Using Lotto Games as the Focus of Their Lotteries, 1993

State	Lotto	Daily Number	Instant	Total
Florida	1.86 (56.7)	.67 (20.5)	.75 (22.7)	3.28
Illinois	1.74 (65.4)	.19 (7.1)	.72 (27.2)	2.65
New York	1.08 (44.0)	1.08 (44.0)	.29 (12.0)	2.45
California	.69 (69.0)	.06 (6)	.25 (25.0)	1.00

Source: Massachusetts Lottery Commission

Strategy 3: The Daily Number Game—Good Pitching, Good Defense

The final way in which a general manager can build his or her baseball team is to use the strategy that the best offense is a good defense. What this strategy requires is that the team have very solid pitching that is backed up by good defense. It takes no unnecessary risks and in essence is waiting for the opponent to make a mistake. While it does not produce the most exciting brand of baseball, it does allow the manager to control the nature of how most games are played. It is certainly the most conservative of the strategies that have been described, but it ought to provide the most consistent results.

Table 4.4 presents the breakdown of lottery proceeds from those states that have used the daily number as the primary focus of their lottery efforts. The table shows the per capita spent per week (1993 figures) on each game, and the figure in parentheses shows the percentage of sales of the total lottery proceeds. (Data in this section provided by the Massachusetts Lottery Commission.)

While the data from this section reveal that all of the lotteries have diversified into the three basic types of games (instant, lotto, and daily number games), they also confirm the fact that each lottery is also pursuing a focus strategy involving one of the games. Each game corresponds to a very definite focus strategy that

Table 4.4
States Using the Daily Number Games as the Focus of
Their Lotteries, 1993

State	Lotto	Daily Number	Instant	Total
D.C.	.84 (17.9)	3.54 (75.9)	.29 (6.1)	4.66
Maryland	.65 (18.4)	2.26 (66.6)	.49 (14.0)	3.40
New Jersey	1.22 (36.3)	1.75 (51.8)	.40 (11.9)	3.37
Pennsylvania	.66 (29.1)	1.36 (56.3)	.33 (14.1)	2.35

Source: Massachusetts Lottery Commission

involves a much different view of its environment. The next section will evaluate the impact and results of these strategies. Again, the criteria for evaluating the successes of a lottery are (1) consistency and (2) future growth possibilities. In the next section, the consistency of each of these strategies will be studied.

PRODUCT LIFE CYCLES OF THE VARIOUS TYPES OF LOTTERY GAMES.

The product life cycle is a marketing concept that identifies four discrete stages that mark the evolution of a product such as a lottery (see Figure 4.1). These stages are useful in determining the correct marketing mix for a product so that revenues can be maximized at each stage. The evolution of products through the product life cycle is well documented. However, whether or not decline must necessarily follow maturation for all products is uncertain. In other words, it may be that this cycle is in fact more of a "system" for certain products. A *cycle* implies that there exists a clear ending point to a product's life. A *system*, on the other hand, implies that a rejuvenation is possible. In a system context, a product could be "repackaged" at maturation and enter into another period of renewal and growth again. Thus, obsolescence would be avoided, and the product life system would begin anew. In this section, we will determine what the life cycle of each lottery is for each game by examining the life cycle for the top two states that are following a niche strategy for

Figure 4.1
Product Life Cycle (System)

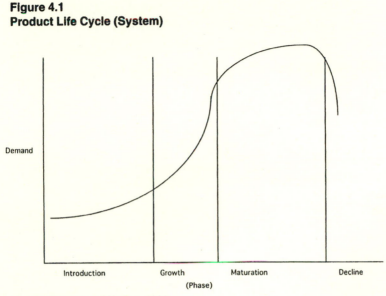

| Introduction | Growth | Maturation | Decline |

(Phase)

Source: Onkvisit and Norton, 1989.

that particular game. By doing this, we will also be able to determine whether that game is capable of renewing itself.

Instant Games

As was pointed out in the previous section, the strategy behind successful instant game lottery sales necessarily involves the constant introduction of new instant games on a seasonal basis. The two states that have had instant games as the focus of their lottery are Massachusetts and Ohio. Figures 4.2 and 4.3 show the quarterly results of instant game sales in these states from 1985 to 1992.

The polynomial equation that describes Massachusetts instant game sales is the following:

$$Y(\text{sales}) = 5.973 + 0.272x + 0.006x^2$$

where

Figure 4.2
Massachusetts Instant Game Sales, 1985–1992

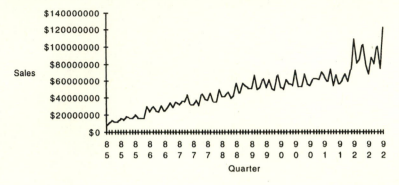

x = quarterly sales

x = 0, January 1985

$p \leq .001$

This equation demonstrates that instant games are certainly on the increase and have not experienced any decline during the period studied.

The polynomial regression equation that describes Ohio instant game sales is the following:

$$Y(\text{sales}) = 3.42 - 0.03x + 0.002x^2$$

where

x = quarterly sales

x = 0, January 1985

$p \leq .005$

Once again, this equation demonstrates that instant games are certainly on the increase and have not experienced any decline during the period studied.

Figure 4.3
Ohio Instant Game Sales, 1985–1992

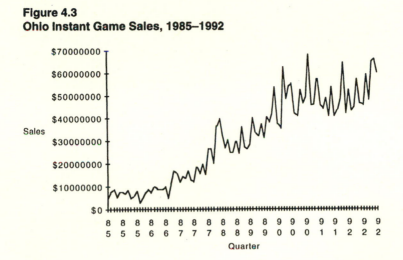

Overall, these results indicate that the instant game strategy is one that can be used to achieve a consistent increase in sales over a long period of time. In fact, Massachusetts has demonstrated that instant game sales can be quite lucrative. It is no coincidence that Massachusetts has the highest per capita lottery in the United States. Hence, it appears that these instant games are still on the growth part of their life cycles. Additionally, it appears that the introduction of new instant games is able to renew sales and interest in this type of lottery game.

Lotto Games

The success of using lotto games as the focal point of a lottery strategy depends upon the frequency of large jackpots, which can stir the public's interest in the games. Obviously, once a series of large jackpots are built up, it is hoped that these bettors will become frequent players of these lotto games. The two most successful states that have used the lotto as the strategic starting point of their lottery operations are Florida and Illinois. Figures 4.4 and 4.5, respectively, show how these lotto games have fared.

Figure 4.4
Florida Lotto Sales, 1988–1992

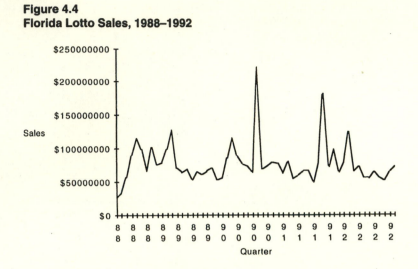

Figure 4.5
Illinois Lotto Sales, 1985–1992

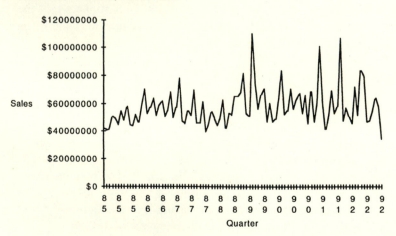

The polynomial regression equation that describes Florida's lotto sales is the following:

$$Y(\text{sales}) = 64.4 + 1.37x - 0.0249x^2$$

where

x = quarterly sales

$x = 0$, January 1988

$p \leq .005$

These results indicate that lotto sales in Florida are on the maturation segment of the product life cycle. Even though Florida has tried to introduce other types of lotto games, these lotto games have not been able to renew interest in the lotto. Hence, the Florida lotto game seems to be on the downward side of the product life cycle.

The polynomial regression equation that describes Illinois's lotto sales is the following:

$$Y(\text{sales}) = 45.9 + 0.428x - 0.00298x^2$$

where

x = quarterly sales

$x = 0$, January 1985

$p \leq .003$

Once again, this equation demonstrates that the Illinois lotto game is clearly on the declining segment of the product life cycle. Like Florida, Illinois has attempted to renew interest in lotto games by offering new types of lotto games, but lotto sales in Illinois still continue to decline slowly.

It appears that even those states with the most successful lotto games have not been able to sustain these games over the long run.

Both of the above results reveal that these lotto games are on the decline segment of the product life cycle. It appears that the public loses interest in lotto games in the long run even if large jackpots occur regularly.

Daily Number Games

The daily number game was characterized earlier as the most conservative lottery game. The lottery that uses this game as its main source of revenue is one that values a steady, consistent stream of revenue. The two most successful lotteries that have used this daily number strategy are the District of Columbia (D.C.) and Maryland. Figures 4.6 and 4.7 demonstrate how these lotteries have fared using the daily number as chief source of revenue.

The regression equation that best describes D.C.'s daily number sales is known as the *random walk*; that is, the best predictor is its average. The mean (average) sales for D.C.'s daily number game is 84.257. In other words, D.C.'s daily number has achieved a steady state. Its product life cycle is nonexistent. On the other hand, D.C.'s daily number is also not experiencing any growth.

The Maryland daily number game, like D.C.'s daily number game, has its regression equation, the random walk; that is, the best predictor is its average. The mean (average) sales for Maryland's daily number game is 47.148. In other words, Maryland's daily number has achieved a steady state, neither growing nor declining.

Overall, the daily number game is remarkably consistent in that its average sales are its best predictor. A daily number game can be counted on to contribute a certain amount of funds, but this amount cannot be increased over the long run. It certainly appears that these two daily number games are on the mature phase of their product life cycles. How long these games will remain on this plateau cannot be determined presently. The other question facing these two lotteries is, Can this daily number be renewed, or is it facing a slow, painful decline? A related question is, Can a state introduce other types of lottery games or dif-

Figure 4.6
District of Columbia's Daily Number Sales, 1985–1992

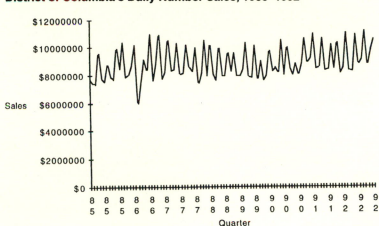

Figure 4.7
Maryland's Daily Number Games, 1985–1992

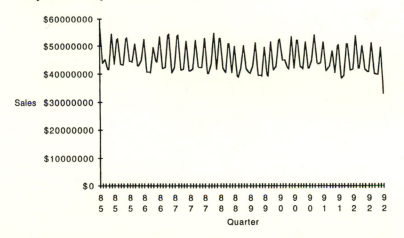

ferent types of gambling using the daily number as the basis for gambling activity?

SUMMARY

The results reveal that instant games are the only type of lottery game capable of sustained growth in the long run. Certainly, Massachusetts, which runs by a wide margin the most successful U.S. lottery, has employed these instant games to their fullest advantage. Why has Massachusetts been so successful in developing these games? One factor has to be the marketing skill of the commission; the demographics (i.e., its diversity) of the Massachusetts population must also be another factor.

There is another interesting aspect to the success of these instant games. Many states that have recently begun lotteries (such as Texas, Minnesota, Iowa, and West Virginia) have used these instant games as their initial offerings. Obviously, they have seen how successful Massachusetts has been in developing these games and have used Massachusetts as the model lottery. It remains to be seen whether the demographics of these states will allow them to emulate Massachusetts's success.

As for the lotto games, even the most successful lotto games (Florida, Illinois) are subject to the product life cycle effect in the long run—that is, providing rapid growth during their inception, but this growth cannot be maintained and eventually sales of these lotto games decline. It has already been noted that the strategy of using the lotto as the focus of a state's lottery sales is one favored by large states. It is interesting to note that when California recently started its lottery, it opted to use the lotto game as its first game. Obviously, the results from this strategy have been disappointing, with per capita sales of only $1.00.

The daily number game was earlier characterized as the most conservative approach to running a lottery. The preceding results confirmed that the daily number game did provide a lottery commissioner with a steady stream of revenue, but it is a stream of income that cannot be increased over the long run. The most successful daily number game appears to be operated by the District of Columbia, where sales are constant but at a consistently high level. It appears that the demographics of D.C. are well suited to the daily number game, that is, almost exclusive urban population. Meanwhile, states such as New York, New Jersey, and Pennsylvania that have many urban centers but that also have a high percentage of their population living in rural or suburban districts have not fared quite as well as D.C. in using the daily number game as the focus of their lottery games. Once again, it still needs to be determined whether the daily number game is one that can be used to introduce other forms of gambling without promoting the cannibalization effect that the introduction of these games would have on existing daily number sales.

Hence, the instant game strategy seems to provide the best basis for long-term growth. However, there are other factors that could change this perception, and these will be examined in the next section.

Future Events and Their Effect on Current Lottery Gaming

So far, it has been established that instant games can be counted on to provide a state steady growth in sales (but certainly not spectacular growth) over the long run. However, if a state is in desperate need of large amounts of additional revenue, instant lottery games do not appear to provide the answer. If the legislature is not willing to raise other forms of taxes and turns to other forms of gambling such as video poker, casino gambling , keno, or even OTB in order to raise revenue, it is commonly believed that cannibalization of existing lottery games will take place. Some maintain that the introduction of either video poker or keno will negatively affect instant game sales. The effect that casino gambling would have on overall lottery sales is also the subject of considerable debate. The extent to which the introduction of other forms of gambling cannibalizes sales of existing lottery games will be studied extensively in the next chapter.

Chapter 5

Lottery Sales and Other Forms of Gambling: Possible Cannibalization and Other Consequences

Since the early 1990s, there has been a marked increase in state sponsorship of all types of gambling. Some of these gambling activities include casino gambling, video poker, offtrack betting, keno, video lottery, and riverboat gambling. The rationale behind the introduction of all these new types of gambling ventures is the same as the one that was used to legitimize the lottery: The ever-increasing need for more state revenue more than supersedes any reservations about the appropriateness of sponsoring additional forms of gambling. Obviously, the gamble here is that the public not only will tolerate but will participate in these additional forms of gambling.

But adding new forms of gambling might prove to be a trickier business than merely getting public approval or tolerance. One common problem that firms face when they introduce new products in a market segment where they already have an existing product is called cannibalization. Cannibalization is the deterioration of one product's (game's) sales as a result of the introduction of another product (game) or, conversely, the increase in sales of one product (game) at the expense of another. A classic example of this phenomenon is the collapse of Miller High-Life beer sales after the introduction of Miller Lite beer. While the new product, Miller Lite, proved to be wildly successful, Miller became synonymous with "Lite" to the detriment of its original beer, "High Life," whose sales fell well over 50 percent. If this cannibalization effect exists between lottery games and other forms of gambling (such as casino gambling, video poker, offtrack betting, and keno), then the overall result of introducing new forms of gambling will be that total revenue will not increase by the amount hoped for, or perhaps, the total revenue will even remain the same after the introduction of this new game. State officials are hoping that gambling revenues are not a zero-sum game but rather a form of entertainment that can be tapped further.

For if these new state-sponsored forms of gambling are to bring in the expected windfall of new revenue for the state's coffers, then the possibility of a possible cannibalization effect on existing lottery games must be examined. In this section, the lottery sales of six states will be analyzed for possible cannibalization of state lottery sales: (1) the introduction of casino gambling in Connecticut in February 1992; (2) Rhode Island's experiment with video poker machines in various locations throughout the state in September 1992; (3) the start of keno drawings in Maryland in January 1993; (4) Pennsylvania's establishment of offtrack betting in January 1988 and permitting sales of small games of chance by nonprofit organizations in January 1991; (5) Oregon's use of video lottery in April 1992; and finally, (6) Iowa's licensing of riverboat gambling in April 1993. In each case, it will be determined whether the introduction of a new form of gambling has an effect on lottery sales and, if it has, which one of the lottery games has been affected by this new form of gambling.

A year's worth of weekly data will be examined. Sales for twenty-six weeks before the introduction of a new form of gambling will be compared with the sales of twenty-six weeks after the introduction of the new form of gambling. The statistical methodology that was employed to determine these outcomes is ARIMA (autoregressive integrated moving average) intervention analysis. For the interested reader, a description of this terminology as well as the results will be included as an appendix to this chapter.

RESULTS

Connecticut and Casino Gambling

On February 15,1992, the Mashantucket Pequot Indians opened the doors to New England's only legal casino at Foxwoods, in Ledyard, Connecticut, after receiving permission from the federal district court. Although this excursion into casino gambling was not initiated by the state of Connecticut, it certainly forced state officials to face two issues: (1) How would the opening of this casino affect the sales of existing lottery games? (2) Should the state open its own casino in order to recoup possible losses in gambling revenues?

To answer the first question, it is helpful to look at the makeup of the Connecticut state lottery. Throughout the period between 1991 and 1992, average Connecticut state lottery sales broke down in the following manner:

Lotto	Daily Number	Instant	Total
1.49	1.17	.70	3.36

Figure 5.1 shows Connecticut's total weekly lottery sales for the period August 20, 1991 (twenty-six weeks before the opening of

Figure 5.1
Connecticut's Total Weekly Lottery Sales,
August 20, 1991, to August 15, 1992

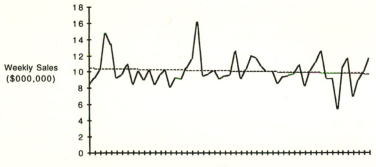

Foxwoods) to August 15, 1992 (twenty-six weeks after the opening of Foxwoods). Examining Figure 5.1, it can be seen that throughout this period Connecticut's total lottery proceeds were declining slightly at a constant rate. This conclusion is also confirmed by the ARIMA intervention analysis; that is, throughout the fifty-two-week study, there was a slight decline in lottery sales. This analysis also showed that the introduction of casino gambling in no way "speeded" up this decline in lottery sales. Perhaps the reason for this finding is that lottery players and casino players do not significantly overlap one another.

Another possible explanation for this result is that Connecticut's lottery was relying on a mix of games that was not capable of sustaining growth; in other words, this mix of games was in the mature or declining segment in its life cycle. Moreover, it appears that Connecticut lottery officials have never developed the potential of instant games, although perhaps the onset of casino gambling precluded a strategy to develop this lottery segment. Therefore, the introduction of casino gambling did not cannibalize existing lottery sales and seems to have had no effect whatsoever on lottery players. But the dilemma facing Connecticut revenue officials was this: With lottery sales declining, were there other forms of gambling that could be instituted in order to increase gambling revenue in a state that had been extremely hard hit by defense spending cutbacks?

One possible answer to this question was for the state to compete with the Mashantucket Pequot Indians by opening its own casino. Various sites for casino gambling were proposed throughout the state. Bridgeport was one possible site for casino gambling, and Hartford was another site, where the recently closed G. Fox Department Store building off I-84 was being considered as a possible building to house this casino venture. Both cities had experienced severe economic downturns in the early 1990s, and hence the argument was made that casinos could make the cities attractive convention centers, thereby providing needed service jobs (*Boston Globe*, July 14, 1992, p. B1).

But the state did have another less risky option. In the court order that permitted the Mashantucket Pequot Indians to open a casino, it was stipulated that they were not allowed to operate slot machines unless the tribe got permission from the state. Hence, one option that Connecticut state officials had was to allow slot machines in the Foxwoods casino but to demand 10 percent of the profits from those machines. This is precisely what state officials did.

This second solution was the one chosen by Connecticut officials for a variety of reasons. First, there would be an increase in state gambling proceeds, albeit not as great as operating its own "successful" casino. Second, this increase in revenue was risk free. Rather than operating its own casino, it was now the Mashantucket Pequot Indians who were risking the threat by neighboring states such as Massachusetts and New York that were, and still are, considering legislation to allow casino gambling in various locations in their respective states. Since it has been estimated that well over 60 percent of the cars in Foxwoods' parking lots are from neighboring states, the argument made by many legislators in these states is a familiar one: Why should our states lose this possible source of revenue to a neighboring state? (*Boston Globe*, January 3, 1993). If people are going to gamble, let them gamble at home. Hence, the New York legislature is constantly debating the merits about permitting casino gambling in the Catskill Mountain region, while the Massachusetts legislature has been entertaining bills permitting casino gambling in Boston Harbor as well as many sites in the western part of the state. Just as the first lottery in New Hampshire spawned a "domino" effect—that is, it led to the establishment of lottery games throughout the rest of the country—it appears that the establishment of the Foxwoods casino in Connecticut might have the same effect.

Rhode Island and Video Poker Machines

Rhode Island's lottery was started in the early 1970s like many of the other state lotteries in the northeastern part of the United States. To compete with surrounding bigger states, in 1992

Rhode Island joined a consortium of fourteen other states plus the District of Columbia in order to be able to offer a competitive (in terms of large jackpots) lotto. Rhode Island also permits jai alai betting.

But to reap even more revenue from gambling activities, on September 30, 1992, the Rhode Island lottery commission began to sponsor video poker machines in various locations throughout the state. Since the only lottery game that Rhode Island runs exclusively is its daily number game, the introduction of video poker games should have its greatest effect on this game.

In viewing Figure 5.2, it is quite apparent that sales of Rhode Island's numbers games have actually increased after the introduction of video poker games. Needless to say, this result is a bit surprising. Once again, it appears that either there is no overlap of players or that residents are spending even more of their funds on gambling activities. This conclusion is also confirmed by the ARIMA intervention analysis; that is, throughout the fifty-two-week study, there was an increase in lottery sales. But this analysis also showed that the introduction of video poker machines in no way intensified this increase in lottery sales.

However, the form of gambling that has been severely negatively affected by the introduction of video poker has been charitable institutions that run bingo games. Fire halls, churches, and

Figure 5.2
Rhode Island's Daily Number Sales, April 1992 to March 1993

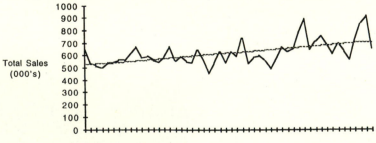

schools that run bingo games to raise money to support their institutions have all reported at least a 50 percent drop in revenue (*Providence Journal*, January 1, 1993). How the state is going to deal with this question remains to be seen. But it has certainly forced these institutions to join antigambling groups in demanding that the state stop expanding its gambling operations and in fact withdraw from them completely.

Maryland and Keno Gambling

On January 3, 1993, Maryland introduced keno gambling to supplement its lottery revenues. Keno is a hybrid of bingo and instant lottery games. Players can choose from one to forty numbers (typically ten). Winnings are based on the correct number of picks. Drawings are usually held every five minutes. Top jackpots typically are $100,000. Currently, there are eight states sponsoring keno: California, Kansas, Maryland, Nebraska, Oregon, Rhode Island, Washington, and West Virginia.

It was indicated previously that Maryland's lottery traditionally had focused on the daily number game. Since keno is played frequently, it appears that the strategy behind the introduction of this type of gambling involves substituting keno for developing an instant game strategy. However, it also remains to be seen how keno would affect the sales of daily number tickets, which had been the "cash cow" of the Maryland lottery.

From Figure 5.3, it is quite obvious that the introduction of keno gambling had a serious negative effect on Maryland's daily number game. While overall lottery revenue increased slightly, the ARIMA intervention analysis confirms that this decline in daily number sales was rapid and permanent. It certainly appears that this form of gambling had cannibalized an existing lottery game so that total overall revenue will eventually go down unless Maryland officials find a way of keeping keno at its current high level of play. One must also wonder whether there is any possible way of increasing interest in keno in the future in order to allow for future growth.

Figure 5.3
Maryland's Daily Number Sales, July 1, 1992, to June 30, 1993

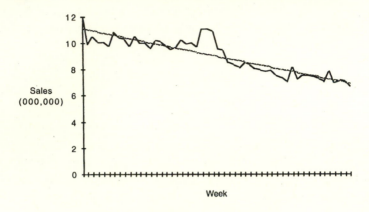

Pennsylvania: Offtrack Betting and Nonprofit Organizations' Games of Chance

OTB and the Daily Number Game. On November 30, 1988, the Pennsylvania legislature overrode Governor Robert Casey's veto and passed an act that authorized offtrack betting sites in the state of Pennsylvania. This act permitted pari-mutuel betting at sites within fifty miles of the track using simulcasts broadcast from various racetracks. The rationale behind the passage of this act was to "revitalize the horse racing" industry, which the Pennsylvania assembly "recognizes is in a state of decline" (Laws of Pennsylvania, Act 1988–127). It was also hoped that these offtrack locations would provide service jobs throughout the state. Since the bets placed at these offtrack location went directly into the pari-mutuel pool at the track, the tracks would also benefit from this increase in betting activity.

It is interesting to note that in the legislation that enabled OTB no consideration was given to what possible effect this activity might have on the Pennsylvania lottery. The Pennsylvania lottery employed a strategy that depended on the daily number to provide the biggest share of sales. In 1989, the breakdown of Pennsylvania lottery sales was:

Lotto	Daily Number	Instant	Total
.63	1.39	.38	2.40

Hence, if OTB had an effect on Pennsylvania lottery sales, it would most likely affect the sales of the daily number game.

Figure 5.4 shows the total weekly sales of Pennsylvania lottery sales from the period July 1, 1987 (twenty-six weeks before the implementation of OTB) to July 1, 1988 (twenty-six weeks after the implementation of OTB). In examining Figure 5.4, it can be ascertained that throughout this time period the Pennsylvania lottery was experiencing overall growth. The driving force behind this growth was the growth of the daily number game. This conclusion is also confirmed by the ARIMA intervention analysis; that is, throughout the fifty-two-week study, there was a slight growth in lottery sales, with the introduction of OTB in no way interfering with this growth. Hence, it appears that the introduction of OTB had no effect on the Pennsylvania lottery in the short run either positively or negatively.

Once again, it appears that the lottery players fail to overlap with other gamblers in significant numbers—or at least they continue to play the lottery at the same rate even with the introduction

Figure 5.4
Pennsylvania's Total Lottery Sales, July 1, 1987, to July 1, 1988
(In millions)

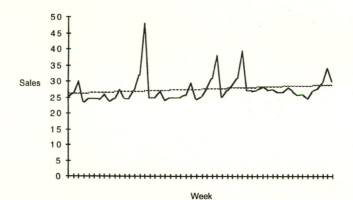

of other forms of gambling. Indeed, total gambling revenue does not seem to be a zero-sum game. Meanwhile, there have been additional sites for OTB opening throughout the state. But this development has not really helped to save horse racing in Pennsylvania (three tracks have closed since the inception of OTB), although it has obviously created service jobs in the communities where the OTB offices are located (*Philadelphia Inquirer*, February 11, 1993, p. D1).

Permitting of Games of "Small Chance" and Daily Number Game. In 1991, Pennsylvania began to permit various nonprofit organizations to engage in selling numerous instant game tickets and small prize games. The argument made in favor of this action was that state-sponsored gambling activities were hurting the fund-raising ability of nonprofit organizations such as churches, volunteer fire companies, and ambulance services. However, lottery officials contended that this action was lessening interest in the state's own lottery games, thereby reducing revenue to the state. Figure 5.5 suggests that since 1991 the Pennsylvania daily number lottery has experienced a slow and gradual decline in sales. The ARIMA intervention analysis also confirms the nega-

Figure 5.5
Pennsylvania's Daily Number Sales, 1985–1992

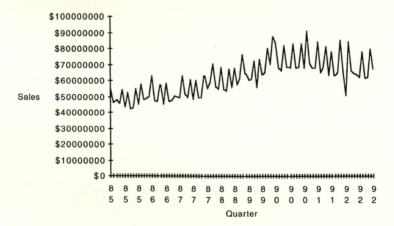

tive effect that the introduction of games of small chance has had on the sale of daily number tickets.

Obviously, the lottery officials were correct in their assessment of how permitting competition of this sort from nonprofit organizations would hurt the state's lottery sales. Yet politically, there was little that lottery officials could do to stop the introduction of this form of gambling.

Oregon and Video Lottery

The state of Oregon has instituted an extremely aggressive lottery/gambling policy. At the beginning of 1992, the Oregon legislature legalized the following gambling initiative:

1. All three segments of the lottery—that is, the daily number, lotto games, and instant games
2. Weekly "pool" betting on professional sports games
3. Keno gambling

The only segments of the gambling industry that Oregon had not authorized were video poker and casino gambling. In April 1992, the Oregon legislature added a rather unique addition to its stable of gambling offerings. At the urging of the Oregon lottery commission, video lottery was legalized. Video lottery was in reality a combination of both video poker games and casino gambling. It enabled lottery players to play on video screens various versions of casino gambling games such as blackjack, poker, and slot machines. In many ways, video lottery was a small casino that was placed in taverns and restaurants. While the video lottery machines certainly did not have the elegance of the surroundings that casino players have become accustomed to, it certainly enabled them to play many of their favorite casino games.

Video Lottery and the Oregon Lottery's Instant Games. If video lottery was to cannibalize any of the existing segments of Oregon's earlier lottery offerings, it would certainly be the instant games segment of the Oregon lottery. The most popular instant games that were being offered throughout the country at that time were also variations of casino games. One example of this phenomenon was an instant ticket game that mimicked the casino game blackjack. The player would buy an instant lottery ticket that would have five blackjack plays on each instant ticket. The player receives $2 for each win on a ticket that costs $1. While the video lottery offers the same playoffs as the instant game version of blackjack, it would certainly seem to simulate the actual casino experience of playing blackjack far better than rubbing a paper ticket.

Before the start of video lottery in April 1992, the breakdown for sales of the various segments of the Oregon lottery were:

Lotto	Daily Number	Instant	Total
.62	.71	.59	1.92

Figure 5.6 shows instant game sales of the Oregon lottery from October 1991 (twenty-six weeks before the start of video lottery) to September 1992 (twenty-six weeks after the start of video lottery).

In examining Figure 5.6, it clearly appears that the instant game segment of the Oregon lottery was declining throughout the period that was studied. The question that needs to be answered is whether

Figure 5.6
Oregon's Total Instant Sales, October 1991 to September 1992

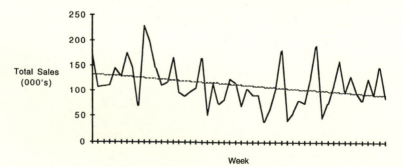

Week

the institution of the video lottery speeded up the decline of the instant games sales. The ARIMA intervention analysis confirms this hypothesis, namely, that the video lottery has hastened the demise of the instant segment of the Oregon lottery. From Figure 5.6, it also appears that with the start of video lottery, the instant game segment of the Oregon lottery became more volatile and unpredictable.

Perhaps Oregon lottery officials were well aware that its instant games segment was stagnant and not capable of further growth, given the number of other lottery games that Oregon was sponsoring at this time. Whatever the rationale that was used to justify the introduction of video lottery, it appears that the instant game segment was sacrificed by officials of the Oregon lottery in order to introduce video lottery. In the next section, it will be determined whether this gamble by Oregon lottery officials has paid in additional overall revenues for the Oregon lottery.

Video Lottery and Oregon's Overall Lottery Sales. The previous section's analysis showed that the introduction of video lottery did indeed cannibalize the sales of the instant game segment of the Oregon lottery. The question that now needs to be answered is whether the revenue from video lottery compensated the Oregon lottery for its loss of instant games revenue. In other words, even if video lottery has cannibalized instant games sales, its introduction could be termed a success if overall lottery revenue for Oregon increased after the introduction of video lottery.

Figure 5.7 shows the overall sales for the Oregon lottery from October 1991 (twenty-six weeks before the start of video lottery) to September 1992 (twenty-six weeks after the start of video lottery).

In examining Figure 5.7, it appears that total revenues for the Oregon lottery were increasing throughout the period that was studied. The question that needs to be answered is whether the institution of the video lottery significantly increased the rate of growth of total lottery sales. The ARIMA intervention analysis confirms this hypothesis, namely, that the video lottery has significantly increased the rate of growth of the Oregon lottery. To reinforce this finding, one only needs to compare the breakdown for sales of the various segments of the Oregon lottery before and after the start of the video lottery game:

Figure 5.7
Oregon's Total Lottery Sales, October 1991 to September 1992

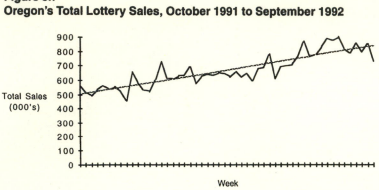

Week

Oregon Lottery Sales as of January 1992

Lotto	Daily Number	Instant	Total
.62	.71	.59	1.92

Oregon Lottery Sales as of January 1993

Lotto	Daily Number	Instant	Video Lottery	Total
.55	.68	.29	.96	2.48

Given these results, there is little doubt that the video lottery game was a financial success. Overall, lottery sales increased by 22.6 percent in a one-year period. Admittedly, it took a large part of the sales for the instant game segment of the Oregon lottery. It remains to be seen if this video lottery game has the potential to maintain this rate of growth or whether lottery games or gambling initiatives can use the video lottery game as a base upon which to build additional gambling revenue.

Iowa and Riverboat Gambling

One of the more interesting developments in the gambling industry has been the upsurge in riverboat gambling activity. The boats are floating casinos that cruise around a given portion of a harbor, river, or lake and then return to port. Unlike a casino, the number of hours that players can gamble is limited. These gambling "cruises" usually include an elegant dinner plus an orchestra that provides music for dancing. Hence, the riverboat has more of an air of "entertainment" and social acceptability than any other form of gambling.

What makes the phenomenon of riverboat gambling even more fascinating is its acceptance by states that do not even sponsor a lottery! For example, Mississippi has established various sites throughout the state for riverboat gambling even though the state itself has not even sanctioned a lottery. Since the gambling industry seeks to obtain and maintain the public's acceptance, the riverboat gambling segment of the industry appears to be one of the safest of all the forms for a state to sponsor. It is now time to examine riverboat gambling's effect when it is introduced into a state that has had a lottery for many years.

Before the start of riverboat gambling in April 1993, the breakdown for sales of the various segments of Iowa's lottery were:

Lotto	Daily Number	Instant	Total
.50	.09	.81	1.40

Figure 5.8 shows Iowa's total proceeds from all segments of the lottery from October 1992 (twenty-six weeks before the start of

Figure 5.8
Iowa's Total Lottery Sales, October 1992 to September 1993

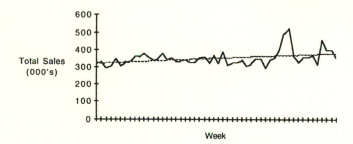

riverboat gambling) to September 1993 (twenty-six weeks after the start of riverboat gambling).

In viewing Figure 5.8, it appears that total sales for Iowa's lottery games have actually increased after the introduction of riverboat gambling. Once again, it appears either that there is no overlap of players or that residents of Iowa or neighboring states are spending even more of their funds on gambling activities. This conclusion is also confirmed by the ARIMA intervention analysis; that is, throughout the fifty-two-week study, there was an increase in lottery sales. But the ARIMA analysis also showed that the introduction of riverboat gambling in no way intensified this increase in lottery sales; that is, riverboat gambling had no effect on lottery sales whatsoever. Hence, riverboat gambling appears to be a form of gambling that does not cannibalize existing lottery sales.

CONCLUSION

The results of this chapter have some interesting implications for developing an overall strategy for state-sponsored gambling activities. It appears that some forms of gambling did not significantly interfere with the existing lottery game, whereas some others did cannibalize existing lottery sales. The three forms of gambling that did negatively affect existing lottery sales were Pennsylvania's permission to nonprofit organizations to sell games of small chance; Maryland's experiment with keno gambling; and finally, Oregon's venture into video lottery. In general, it appears that the public's appetite for gambling is not a zero-sum game but can be expanded further. How far this expansion can go is something that policy makers as well as lottery commissioners have to ascertain.

This expansion has to take into account the many side effects that previous expansions into the gambling arena did not take into account. Connecticut's experience with casino gambling was tempered by its anticipation of countermeasures by neighboring states. Casino gambling seems to be subject to the "slippery slope" argument; that is, once a state decides to permit it, then every state is pressured to adapt it. Currently, major cities such as Boston,

Chicago, New Orleans, and Philadelphia are all petitioning their respective state legislatures for the right to institute casino gambling in order to make their cities a more attractive site for conventions. However, one must ask the question, If every major city ends up sponsoring casino gambling, what advantage would it be to that city in attracting conventions? Rhode Island's use of video poker had the unforeseen effect of ruining bingo as a fund-raising tool for nonprofit organizations.

We have also seen how the Pennsylvania legislature's desire to help nonprofit organizations has led to the decline in the lottery as a source of revenue for the state. A similar fate happened to Maryland's daily number when Maryland ventured into keno gambling. However, while Oregon's video lottery did indeed cannibalize an existing segment of its lottery—namely, instant games—overall lottery revenue dramatically increased. What all of these outcomes point out is the need for a state to develop an overall strategy as it approaches the tempting revenue stream that new gambling initiatives offer to revenue-hungry state legislators.

In evaluating whether new gambling initiatives fit into a state's overall gambling strategy, various factors or criteria must be taken into account: (1) the need for additional revenue and the ability of the gambling initiative to provide this revenue; (2) the tolerance level of the population for more gambling; (3) the life cycle of various lottery games; (4) the possibility of cannibalizing existing sales; and (5) the establishment of a commission to regulate and control all of the state's gambling activities. Obviously, the answers to these factors are not mutually exclusive. In the next chapter, these criteria will be used in examining, in great detail, the overall gambling strategies of two states, Massachusetts and Pennsylvania.

APPENDIX: ARIMA RESULTS

Intervention analysis requires the identification of an autoregressive integrated moving average (ARIMA) model that replicates each time series analyzed. In ARIMA notation, a model is specified with two shorthand descriptors, (p,d,q) and (P,D,Q). The first element (p) delineates the autoregressive term, the second element (d) is the degree of differencing required to achieve stationarity, and the third term (q) is the extent to which moving average component is associated with the random shocks. The second notational array (P,D,Q) designates analogous terms, except these are associated with seasonality. The ARIMA model is tested against observed series until a statistically adequate model is identified. Adequacy of the model is confirmed after an examination of the autocorrelation function and partial autocorrelation function of the series and when a statistical analysis of the residuals indicates that they constitute a time series of white noise (Ljung, 1978). When an appropriate ARIMA model is specified, it is used to filter that series. At this point, a dynamic model consistent with the postulated intervention effect is formulated. This dynamic model corresponds to the hypothesis because its formulation specifies the configured change in the level of white noise produced by the intervention. Once formulated, the dynamic model is fitted to the residual series, its parameters are estimated, and each is evaluated using the technique suggested by Box and Tiao (1975).

Connecticut and Casino Gambling

The time series for Connecticut's total lottery proceeds was identified as ARIMA model $(0,1,1)$ $(0,1,1)_{12}$. Regular and seasonal differencing achieved stationarity (i.e., the series is centered around the mean). The MA (moving average) parameters were estimated and statistically tested with the following results:

$$\theta = -.032 \ (t = -17.24), \ \theta_{12} = -.41 (t = -2.87)$$

The dynamic model postulated was

$$Y_t = [\omega B/(1 - \delta B)]S_t^{(T)}$$

where ω and δ represent the level of change and the rate of change, respectively. Y_t is the lottery proceeds (filtered series), B is the backspace operator used to achieve stationary mean and variance, and $S_t^{(T)}$ is the binary variable that introduces the intervention into the series. This model is consistent with the hypothesis of a gradual decrease in lottery proceeds due to the introduction of casino gambling. The parameters estimates are

$$\delta = -.41 \ (t = -.21) \text{ and } \omega = 178.9 \ (t = -.40)$$

Since neither value is statistically significant, it appears that the introduction of casino gambling had no significant negative effect on lottery sales in Connecticut either in the short run or in the long run.

Rhode Island and Video Poker Games

The time series for Rhode Island total lottery proceeds was identified as ARIMA model $(1,1,0) \ (0,1,0)_{12}$. Regular and seasonal differencing achieved stationarity (i.e., the series is centered around the mean). The AR (autoregressive) parameters were estimated and statistically tested with the following results:

$$\phi = .74 \ (t = 9.42)$$

This model indicates that total lottery sales were actually increasing throughout the time period that was analyzed.

The dynamic model postulated was

$$Y_t = [\omega B/(1 - \delta B)]S_t^{(T)}$$

where ω and δ represent the level of change and the rate of change, respectively. Y_t is the lottery proceeds (filtered series), B is the backspace operator used to achieve stationary mean and variance, and $S_t^{(T)}$ is the binary variable that introduces the intervention into the series. This model is consistent with the hypothesis of a gradual decrease in lottery proceeds due to the introduction of video poker. The parameters estimates are

$\phi = 8.76 \ (t = .541)$ and $\omega = 9.5 \ (t = .690)$

Since both parameters are positive, one might make a case that the introduction of video poker actually increased the total sales of lottery tickets in Rhode Island. However, since neither value is statistically significant, the ARIMA analysis would suggest that the introduction of video poker games had no significant effect on lottery sales in Rhode Island.

Maryland and Keno Gambling

The time series for Maryland's total lottery proceeds was identified as ARIMA model $(1,1,1) \ (0,1,0)_{12}$. Regular and seasonal differencing achieved stationarity (i.e., the series is centered around the mean). The AR and MA parameters were estimated and statistically tested with the following results:

$\phi = -.43 \ (t = -7.93), \ \theta = -.62 \ (t = -6.24)$

The dynamic model postulated was

$Y_t = [\omega B/(1 - \delta B)]S_t^{(T)}$

where ω and δ represent the level of change and the rate of change, respectively. Y_t is the lottery proceeds (filtered series), B is the backspace operator used to achieve stationary means and variance, and $S_t^{(T)}$ is the binary variable that introduces the intervention into the series. This model is consistent with the hypothesis of a gradual decrease in lottery proceeds due to the introduction of keno gambling. The parameters estimates are

$\delta = -2.31 \ (t = -3.21)$ and $\omega = -85.9 \ (t = -4.10)$

Since both values are statistically significant, it appears that the introduction of keno gambling had a significant negative effect on lottery sales in Maryland in both the short run and the long run.

Pennsylvania: Offtrack Betting and Games of Small Chance

Offtrack Betting and the Daily Number Game. The time series for Pennsylvania's daily number lottery sales was identified as ARIMA model $(1,1,0)(0,1,0)_{12}$. Regular and seasonal differencing achieved stationarity (i.e., the series is centered around the mean). The AR parameters were estimated and statistically tested with the following results:

$$\phi = .45 \; (t = 5.48)$$

These results indicate that Pennsylvania's daily number game was actually increasing at a slow but steady pace throughout the period studied.

The dynamic model postulated was

$$Y_t = [\omega B/(1 - \delta B)]S_t^{(T)}$$

where ω and δ represent the level of change and the rate of change, respectively. Y_t is the lottery proceeds (filtered series), B is the backspace operator used to achieve stationary mean and variance, and $S_t^{(T)}$ is the binary variable that introduces the intervention into the series. This model is consistent with the hypothesis of a gradual decrease in lottery proceeds due to the introduction of offtrack betting. The parameters estimates are

$$\phi = .76 \; (t = .541) \text{ and } \omega = 9.5 \; (t = .690)$$

Since neither value is statistically significant, it can be asserted that the introduction of offtrack betting had no significant negative effect on daily number lottery sales in Pennsylvania.

Games of Small Chance for Nonprofits and Total Lottery Sales. The time series for Pennsylvania's total lottery proceeds was identified as ARIMA model $(1,1,0)(1,1,0)_{12}$. Regular and seasonal differencing achieved stationarity (i.e., the series is centered around the mean). The AR parameters were estimated and statistically tested with the following results:

$$\phi = -.43 \ (t = -6.33), \ \phi_{12} = -.07 \ (t = 2.34)$$

The dynamic model postulated was

$$Y_t = [\omega B/(1 - \delta B)]S_t^{(T)}$$

where ω and δ represent the level of change and the rate of change, respectively. Y_t is the lottery proceeds (filtered series), B is the backspace operator used to achieve stationary mean and variance, and $S_t^{(T)}$ is the binary variable that introduces the intervention into the series. This model is consistent with the hypothesis of a gradual decrease in lottery proceeds due to the introduction of nonprofit gambling. The parameters estimates are

$$\delta = -3.11 \ (t = -2.86) \text{ and } \omega = -45.9 \ (t = -3.11)$$

Since both values are statistically significant, it appears that the introduction of nonprofit gambling had a significant negative effect on daily number lottery sales in Pennsylvania in both the short run and the long run.

Oregon and Video Lottery

Video Lottery and Instant Games. The time series for the sales of Oregon's instant lottery game was identified as ARIMA model $(1,2,1) \ (0,1,0)_{12}$. Regular and seasonal differencing achieved stationarity (i.e., the series is centered around the mean). The AR and MA parameters were estimated and statistically tested with the following results:

$$\phi = -.34 \ (t = -5.84), \ \theta = -.62 \ (t = -5.75)$$

The dynamic model postulated was

$$Y_t = [\omega B/(1 - \delta B)]S_t^{(T)}$$

where ω and δ represent the level of change and the rate of change, respectively. Y_t is the instant games sales (filtered series), B is the backspace operator used to achieve stationary mean and variance, and $S_t^{(T)}$ is the binary variable that introduces the intervention into the series. This model is consistent with the hypothesis of a gradual decrease in instant games sales due to the introduction of video lottery. The parameters estimates are

$$\delta = -1.07 \ (t = -2.84) \text{ and } \omega = -55.7 \ (t = -3.13)$$

Since both values are statistically significant, it appears that the introduction of video lottery had a significant negative effect on the sales of instant lottery tickets in Oregon in the short run and in the long run.

Video Lottery and Total Lottery Proceeds. The time series for the sales of Oregon's total lottery sales was identified as ARIMA model $(0,1,1) \ (0,1,1)_{12}$. Regular and seasonal differencing achieved stationarity (i.e., the series is centered around the mean). The MA parameters were estimated and statistically tested with the following results:

$$\theta = .52 \ (t = 3.53), \ \theta_{12} = .63 \ (t = 2.76)$$

These results indicate that Oregon's total lottery proceeds were increasing throughout the time series for these sales.

The dynamic model postulated was

$$Y_t = [\omega B/(1 - \delta B)]S_t^{(T)}$$

where ω and δ represent the level of change and the rate of change, respectively. Y_t is the instant games sales (filtered series), B is the backspace operator used to achieve stationary mean and variance, and $S_t^{(T)}$ is the binary variable that introduces the intervention into the series. This model is consistent with the hypothesis of a gradual decrease in instant games sales due to the introduction of video lottery. The parameters estimates are

$$\delta = 1.707 \ (t = 3.78) \text{ and } \omega = 2.9 \ (t = .85)$$

These results indicate that although there was not a statistically significant increase initially resulting from the introduction of the video lottery [$\omega = 2.9 \ (t = .85)$], in the long run, the video lottery did significantly increase total revenue for Oregon's lottery.

Iowa and Riverboat Gambling

The time series for Iowa's total lottery proceeds was identified as ARIMA model $(1,1,0) \ (1,1,0)_{12}$. Regular and season differencing achieved stationarity (i.e., the series is centered around the mean). The AR parameters were estimated and statistically tested with the following results:

$$\phi = .64 \ (t = 5.47), \ \phi_{12} = .13 \ (t = 7.24)$$

This model indicates that total lottery sales were actually increasing throughout the time period that was analyzed.

The dynamic model postulated was

$$Y_t = [\omega B/(1 - \delta B)]S_t^{(T)}$$

where ω and δ represent the level of change and the rate of change, respectively. Y_t is the lottery proceeds (filtered series), B is the backspace operator used to achieve stationary mean and variance, and $S_t^{(T)}$ is the binary variable that introduces the intervention into the series. This model is consistent with the hypothesis of a gradual decrease in lottery proceeds due to the introduction of riverboat gambling. The parameters estimates are

$$\phi = 2.09 \ (t = .639) \text{ and } \omega = 9.5 \ (t = .472)$$

Since both parameters are positive, one might make a case that the introduction of riverboat gambling actually increased the total sales of lottery tickets in Iowa. However, since neither value is statistically significant, the ARIMA analysis would suggest that the introduction of riverboat gambling had no significant effect on lottery sales in Iowa.

Chapter 6

The Expansion of State-Sponsored Gambling Activities: The Cases of Massachusetts and Pennsylvania

In the previous chapter, criteria were established that form the basis for evaluating a state's overall gambling strategy. These criteria were designed to measure how a particular overall gambling plan or policy was meeting the two goals of satisfying the state's needs for additional revenue and the public's concern over additional state involvement in gambling.

This chapter will present two case studies that will examine and evaluate the overall gambling strategies that have been employed by Massachusetts and Pennsylvania. Massachusetts was chosen because it is currently conducting the most successful lottery in the United States (at least in terms of per capita spending). And because of its success, its gambling strategy not only will be closely watched but most likely will be emulated by a number of states. Meanwhile, Pennsylvania operates one of the oldest lotteries in the United States, with the first lottery games starting play in 1972. Hence, the Pennsylvania lottery will give public policy makers of states that began lotteries in the 1980s and later a scenario of decisions and strategies they are likely to face in the future.

These case studies will first analyze the current status of the various lottery games in each of these states by using the trend equation for each game to locate where the game is on its product life cycle. Next, the various strategic gambling options will be cataloged—that is, determining the status of the various gambling options such as keno, video poker, OTB, and casino gambling for Massachusetts and Pennsylvania. After describing the various economic options, the discussion will turn to the political dimension of gambling by describing the reaction of the governors and state legislatures to these proposals. Finally, a summary will be presented that will include a scenario of likely changes in the future gambling strategies of Massachusetts and Pennsylvania.

MASSACHUSETTS

The Massachusetts lottery has generally been acknowledged as a lottery that has been innovative in the strategy that it employs in introducing new games, especially a variety of instant games. The advertising strategy that the Massachusetts lottery commission has employed has also been acknowledged as one of the more innovative and aggressive: Whereas the majority of advertising for state lotteries emphasizes the "good" causes that lottery proceeds support, Massachusetts instead portrays the games as interesting and a normal activity for players to engage in.

Proceeds from the Massachusetts lottery are earmarked to provide state aid to towns and cities. Hence, it is somewhat ironic that just as the New Federalism forced states to adopt lotteries in order to come up with funds that the federal government had previously given to states, now Massachusetts was forcing its local towns and cities to become dependent on lottery proceeds in order to provide basic local services such as police and fire protection.

The Current Status of the Massachusetts Lottery

As was pointed out in Chapter 4, the Massachusetts lottery has been one of the most successful lotteries operated in the United States. The Massachusetts lottery is unique because it uses the instant game as the cornerstone of its lottery operation and appears much more willing to introduce new instant games at a far greater rate than all other lotteries. Currently, the Massachusetts lottery has games in all three lottery segments, that is, instant games, lotto games, and daily number games. Figures 6.1, 6.2 and 6.3 show quarterly sales figures for the three games from 1985 to 1992.

The equation that describes the trend for Massachusetts instant game sales (Figure 6.1) is the following:

$$Y(\text{sales}) = 5.973 + 0.272x + 0.006x^2$$

where:

x = quarters

x = 0, January 1985

$p \leq .001$

This equation demonstrates that instant games are certainly on the increase throughout the time period studied and have not experienced any decline during this time period.

The equation that describes the trend for Massachusetts lotto game sales (Figure 6.2) is the following:

$$Y(\text{sales}) = 24.9 - 3.45x - 0.34x^2$$

Figure 6.1
Massachusetts's Instant Game Sales, 1985–1992

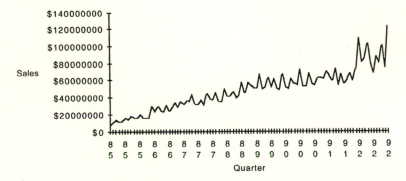

Figure 6.2
Massachusetts's Lotto Sales, 1985–1992

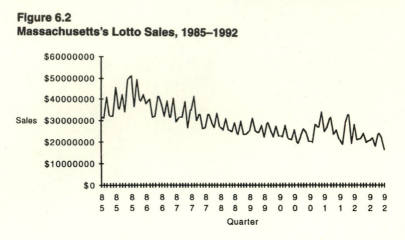

where

x = quarters

x = 0, January 1985

$p \le .04$

This equation confirms what Figure 6.2 seems to indicate—
namely, that sales of lotto game tickets have been on the decrease
throughout the period, and the lottery commission has not found a
way to revive interest in these games.

The equation that describes the trend for Massachusetts daily
number game sales (Figure 6.3) is the following:

$$Y(\text{sales}) = 35 + 1.72x - 0.54x^2$$

where:

x = quarters

x = 0, January 1985

$p \le .04$

Figure 6.3
Massachusetts's Daily Number Sales, 1985–1992

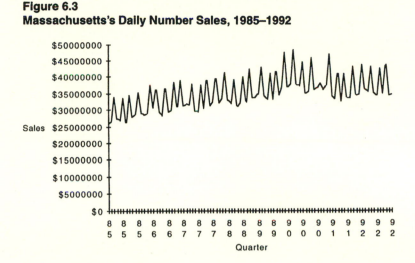

This equation demonstrates that the daily number games have recently experienced a decrease in sales after having gradually increased at the beginning of this series of sales data.

This analysis of Massachusetts lottery sales reveals that the only area that is experiencing gains in sales is the instant games category. The lotto games have experienced a steady and steep decline, while the daily number game appears to have begun a slow but steady decline in sales. Hence, the growth of the Massachusetts lottery is dependent on the growth of a single segment of the market, namely, the instant games. The growth of these instant games has not been able to generate interest in Massachusetts's other lottery offerings, as they continue their declines. Growth in instant games sales will have to serve two functions:

1. Provide the basis to "make up" revenue due to the decline of both the lotto and daily number segments of the lottery; and
2. Provide any growth in overall lottery sales in the event that the governor and the legislature turn to the lottery for additional revenue.

It remains to be seen if instant games can provide the kind of growth that appears to be necessary if the lottery is to fulfill its revenue projections.

Strategic Options for New Gambling Initiatives in Massachusetts

Certainly one of the strategic options for Massachusetts officials was to maintain the status quo and ride out the product life cycles of the various lottery games. But given the results of the previous section, both the executive and legislative branches of government in Massachusetts are well aware that additional gambling opportunities need to be legalized if gambling is to continue to be a consistent source of revenue for the state.

To formulate an overall gambling strategy for Massachusetts, public policy makers had to take into account both internal as well as external influences on its gambling operations. The internal influences result from the political process that must deal with the need of both the executive and legislative branches to control gambling revenue. Meanwhile, the external influences on formulating an overall gambling policy are economic and come from bordering states; that is, the gambling policies of neighboring states in large measure influence another state's gambling strategy. These two forces will now be examined.

Internal Political Environment: Raising More Revenue. In 1993, the Massachusetts economy was starting to recover from the worst recession since the end of World War II. William Weld, the Republican governor of Massachusetts, had been elected on the platform of cutting government spending as well as promising that his administration would not raise taxes. His "libertarian" philosophy of the least government is the best amount of government also fit quite well into his sponsorship of gambling activities. But in order to sponsor his school choice program, Governor Weld needed to find some way of generating additional revenues.

Moreover, most of the state's economists were in agreement that the imposition of any increase in either the sales tax or income tax would wreak havoc on the fragile recovery of the Massachusetts economy. While most politicians profess to be uncomfortable with gambling, the lure of additional revenue as well as the creation of jobs from new gambling enterprises becomes too strong to resist. Moreover, the Massachusetts lottery has been a consistent and growing source of revenue for the state, with the lottery contributing a little over $529 million yearly to the state treasury. However, with grim financial projections for the coming years, state officials hoped that this figure could be expanded eventually to $1 billion out of a total state budget of $13 billion. But to accomplish this goal, both executive and legislative leaders realized that they would have to push for other kinds of gambling opportunities. State Representative Michael Walsh, Massachusetts House chairman of the legislature's Government Regulation Committee, acknowledged this by saying, "This [state-sponsored gambling] is probably the largest nontax revenue source we can tap; if it doesn't happen this year, it will probably have to happen next year as a matter of practical necessity" (*Boston Herald*, December 4, 1992, p. 15).

External Political Environment: Coveting Your Neighbor's Revenue. Another argument frequently used to justify additional gambling ventures by a state government centers around the "Keep the money at home" theme. Again, the comments of Michael Walsh are instructive: "We've done everything we can do to cut costs and raise revenue. There's no place to go except gaming. And if we don't do it in the next five years, we're going to be the last ones to do it" (*Boston Globe*, January 3, 1993, p. 16). To understand State Representative Walsh's concern, it will be instructive to see what options other surrounding states had taken or were proposing to undertake in the future (see Table 6.1).

One can comment on this table from both a vertical and a horizontal perspective. From the vertical perspective, it appears that both the lottery and pari-mutuel betting have become "acceptable" forms of gambling, while casino gambling and video poker are forms of gambling that are attracting a great deal of interest by state officials.

From the horizontal perspective, it is quite apparent from the table that certain states have become much more aggressive in per-

Table 6.1
New England's Gambling Options: What's Being Played and
What's Being Proposed

State	Casino	Jai alai	Keno	Lottery	OTB	Pari-mutuel	Video Poker
Connecticut	X	X	--	X	X	X	*
Maine	*	--	--	X	--	X	*
Massachusetts	*	--	*	X	*	X	*
New Hampshire	*	--	--	X	--	X	*
Rhode Island	*	X	X	X	*	X	X
Vermont	—	--	--	X	--	X	--

X = Already being played

-- = Not being played

* = Proposed

mitting and encouraging state-sponsored gambling activities. There also appears to be a correlation between the severity of the recent recession and the amount of gambling being encouraged. The two states that seem to have the least aggressive gambling policies are Maine and Vermont, whose economies have not suffered nearly as much as those of the other New England states. Meanwhile, the economies of Connecticut and Rhode Island have been particularly hard hit by defense cutbacks as well as failures of various financial institutions in those states. So in order to keep state services at some acceptable minimum, governors of both these states were forced to accept almost every conceivable gambling initiative. As we saw in the previous chapter, these initiatives were for the most part successful in raising additional revenue for the state. Hence, Massachusetts, where support for additional gambling opportunities seems to be building, certainly did not want to be left behind in an area where it had traditionally been a leader.

Massachusetts's Options: Keno, Casino Gambling, OTB, and Video Poker

To meet both the need to raise more revenue for current programs and the challenge posed by its neighboring states to its
future gambling revenue, Massachusetts officials proposed a variety of different gambling proposals. Two of the proposals came
from the executive branch (keno and casino gambling), while the
other two proposals were offered by state legislators (video poker
and offtrack betting). What will follow is a review of what happened to these proposals.

Keno. In the early part of 1993, the Massachusetts lottery commission started to investigate the possibility of starting keno gambling as part of the state lottery commission's stable of games.
Since keno is a combination of bingo and instant lottery games,
the commission assumed that it could institute this game as long as
it informed the appropriate legislative committees. However, State
Senator Thomas Norton had a quite different opinion of this matter. For Senator Norton, keno gambling was a dual issue: (1) In the
senator's opinion, this new form of gambling had to be approved
by the legislature—not just informed that it was going to take
place; (2) but even more significant to the senator was the question
of *who* would control the funds that this new form of gambling
would generate. Previously, lottery games were targeted for specific purposes: Revenues from the daily number and instant games
were designated as revenue provided by the state for use by local
towns and cities. Meanwhile, the lotto games were originally
designed to fund the arts in the state, but revenues from these
games proved to be much more ample than originally anticipated.
Thus, the funds generated by these games for the arts were
"capped" at a million-dollar level, and the rest of the revenue went
into the state's general fund.

How was this issue resolved? Keno gambling was approved by
the state legislature, and the lottery commissioner agreed to seek
the approval of the legislature before instituting any new gambling
initiatives. Keno games would be allowed in any location where

lottery tickets are currently sold, that is, corner stores, bars, restaurants. However, the revenues generated from keno gambling were to go directly into the general state treasury, and so they were not earmarked for any specific purpose.

Casino Gambling. We have seen earlier that the impetus for casino gambling in Massachusetts has been the opening of the Foxwoods casino in Connecticut. In July 1993, Governor Weld, a Republican, added his support for casino gambling in Boston Harbor. His reasoning was quite simple: Governor Weld had proposed that a new "Megaplex" be built in Boston in order to adequately house the city's sports teams, particularly the Patriots (football) and the Red Sox (baseball). Originally when Weld proposed the Megaplex, he wanted to finance this structure by using state bonds. However, the leaders of the Democratic-controlled legislature, Senate President William Bulger and Speaker of the Massachusetts House of Representatives Charles Flaherty, rejected this proposal, saying that taxpayers should not be asked to subsidize profitable sports teams. But the governor maintained that these teams brought the area needed revenue and was determined to build the Megaplex. So he turned to the only other source of revenue available to him to finance the Megaplex, casino gambling. Governor Weld also argued that casino gambling would make Boston a more attractive convention center as well as keeping Massachusetts gamblers at home.

As of April 1994, the issue of the Megaplex as well as casino gambling has not been settled. This linking of the two issues was an interesting political move by Governor Weld. Whereas his proposal for keno gambling left the use of the funds to be decided by the treasurer, revenue from casino gambling was earmarked for a definite purpose. So far, the legislative leaders have not budged in their opposition to casino gambling or the Megaplex. However, it will be interesting to see how these legislative leaders will react if either the Patriots or the Red Sox threaten to leave Boston if the Megaplex is not built. Essentially, there are three options: (1) Let the teams leave the area and hope to withstand the outrage of fans; (2) support some sort of tax increase along with bonds to finance the Megaplex; or (3) give in to the governor and permit casino gambling in order to finance the Megaplex. There is no doubt what the easiest choice would be. Certainly, if one could place a bet on the possibility of casino gambling in Massachusetts in the near future, the odds will certainly favor it.

Offtrack Betting. Unlike the previous two gambling proposals, OTB was not proposed by the Weld administration. Supporters of this gambling initiative in the state legislature had hoped to help the few horse racing tracks left in the state while, of course, raising additional revenue for the state.

But this proposal has received neither much support nor opposition. One reason for this is that the type of racing that has been most successful in Massachusetts has been dog racing. Since the majority of legislators realize that the amount of revenue that could be raised through OTB (for horse racing) is minimal, this proposal has never made it beyond committee. It appears that a gambling proposal needs to have a broad base of support in order to generate the needed interest to ensure its passage. The next gambling proposal, video poker machines, has provoked much more broad-base support; however, it is one that appears to be much more controversial.

Video Poker Machines. In the previous chapter, Rhode Island's experiment with video poker machines in 1992 was highlighted. Rhode Island restricted the placement of video poker machines to racetracks and a few designated "parlors" opened by the lottery commission.

In Massachusetts, proposals for establishing video poker at racetracks were filed in the legislature early in 1993. However, legislators from the section of Massachusetts that was nearest Rhode Island were clamoring to expand the scope of video poker games for Massachusetts by allowing video poker games to be placed not only at racetracks but also in bars and restaurants.

Immediately, there was a negative reaction to this proposal that was led ironically by supporters of the pari-mutuel racetracks. The supporters of this industry were more than willing to support this type of gambling as long as its play was limited to racetracks.

However, once the scope of video poker gaming was to be expanded to all forms of public entertainment, supporters of this industry pointed out the devastating consequences that video poker would have on horse and dog racing industries. Hence, the proposal was killed, but no doubt it will be resurrected as soon as sufficient broad-base support can be assembled.

Conclusion

From this analysis, most of the political forces in Massachusetts's government agreed on the state's need to raise additional nontax revenue. Both the executive and legislative branches agreed with this conclusion, and both used the following arguments to generate public support for new gambling ventures:

1. The need to raise more revenue for good causes and
2. The need to provide Massachusetts residents with games that are available in nearby states so that the revenue stays "home."

However, what Massachusetts public policy makers disagreed on was the appropriate means for carrying out their gambling policy. After all of the political maneuvering and posturing over various gambling proposals, keno gambling has surfaced as the first additional form of gambling to supplement lottery games as a source of state income. Why was keno the sole survivor of this political and economic process? At the end of Chapter 5, five criteria were formulated to evaluate the success or failure of a state's overall gambling strategy. Hence, it would be helpful to review these criteria as a way of understanding why a particular gambling measure succeeded or failed to be enacted.

Keno was the one gambling proposal that was able to fulfill all five criteria in formulating a successful gambling strategy. First, all of the stakeholders (legislature, governor, the public) agreed that the state was in need of additional revenue. It also appeared that keno was capable of providing a significant portion of this needed revenue. Second, keno gambling was considered a tolerable form of gambling. Keno had already been adopted by a neighboring state, which gave it a sense of legitimacy. Keno's format, which is a combination of bingo and lottery, also makes it less controversial than other forms of gambling. Third, both the daily number and lotto games were experiencing gradual declines that did not appear to be reversible. Hence, Massachusetts needed to replace these games if the stream of revenue from the lottery was going to be sustained. Fourth, while keno certainly appears to be a game that could cannibalize instant games sales, the case was made that this form of gambling had much greater potential than instant games in the "long run." Hence, the introduction of keno gambling was a rather risky but proactive strategy. Instant games had proven their worth and had made the Massachusetts lottery the most successful. But the Massachusetts lottery commissioner, Eric Turner, had decided to take the bold step of introducing a new form of gambling rather than "riding out" the life cycle of instant games. Finally, the introduction of keno gambling did not require the establishment of any new commission or a political battle about who would control this type of gambling. Funds were earmarked for the general fund, thus averting any undue political controversy over control of the game or funds.

Meanwhile, all of the other gambling initiatives went down to defeat, at least during this round of proposed gambling initiatives. Certainly, casino gambling could have provided the state with additional revenue, but the linking of this revenue with the building of a new sports arena (Megaplex) for the Boston area proved to be its downfall. The reason for this is that legislators from the rest of the state had nothing to gain from casino gambling. In addition, it appears that the "ethical tolerance" level for casino gambling had not yet been reached. Meanwhile, OTB was passed over as a source of additional gambling revenue for one simple reason: It wouldn't raise sufficient revenues to fund even the most minimal of programs. It had no great opposition nor support and hence lawmakers were not interested in defending this measure. Finally, the introduction of video poker machines into Massachusetts failed because its scope became too wide. Backers of expanded video poker had intended to set up their own commission in order to use the revenue to fund their own purposes. Fellow legislators became suspicious of video poker for two reasons: (1) Just how was this new commission to be set up? (2) Who would control the funds that emanated from it? It also appears that the tolerance level for video poker had not been reached because backers expanded its reach too far and too fast. But Massachusetts was just one of many states that were faced with the issue of expanding gambling opportunities for their constituents. Another state that was also facing various gambling proposals was Pennsylvania. The outcome of Pennsylvania's debate over additional gambling opportunities ought to provide an interesting comparison.

PENNSYLVANIA

Pennsylvania's lottery, which was established in 1972, is one that has used the daily number as its chief source of lottery revenue. Although Pennsylvania has all three segments of the lottery industry, lottery officials have been instructed to spend much less of a percentage of their take on advertising and promotion of lottery activities. Most of Pennsylvania's lottery advertising reminds players that proceeds benefit senior citizens but avoids in general making the games "attractive." These benefits include (1) subsidizing and greatly reducing fares on public transportation throughout the state for senior citizens and (2) making drugs available to senior citizens at greatly reduced costs as well as reducing the cost of many other Medicare costs.

Benefits to senior citizens is the ideal "good" cause for a lottery that is using the daily number game as its primary market segment for two reasons: The median age of Pennsylvania's population is higher than the U.S. median population and the game of choice for older citizens is the daily number. Hence, senior citizens are playing a game that in turn supports themselves. But for Pennsylvania's politicians, the lottery has become a political and economic necessity in satisfying the needs of older Pennsylvanians who constitute a very strong political force in Pennsylvania.

The Current Status of Pennsylvania's Lottery

Like many of the older lotteries in the Northeast, the Pennsylvania lottery is built around the daily number game. The goal of this type of strategic management of a lottery is to achieve a slow but steady growth. In trying to achieve this goal of slow, steady growth, it is also hoped that the lottery will be perceived as an innocuous form of entertainment that should receive maximum tolerance of this type of gambling activity. Currently, Pennsylvania operates games in all three lottery segments. Refer to Figures 6.4, 6.5, and 6.6 for quarterly sales for each type of game from 1985 to 1992.

The equation that describes the trend for Pennsylvania's instant games sales (Figure 6.4) is the following:

$$Y(\text{sales}) = 19.8 + 0.7x - 0.41x^2$$

where:

x = quarters

x = 0, January 1985

$p \leq .07$

Figure 6.4
Pennsylvania's Instant Game Sales, 1985–1992

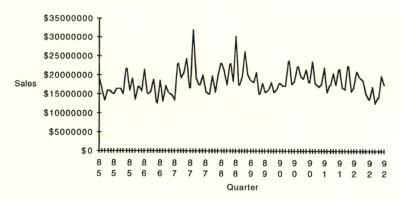

This equation demonstrates that lottery sales of instant game tickets were on the rise in the early part of the sales series but were declining during the later part of the time period studied. It also appears that lottery officials have not been able to regenerate interest in these instant games.

The equation that describes the trend for Pennsylvania's lotto games sales (Figure 6.5) is the following:

$$Y(\text{sales}) = 25.4 - 1.17x - 0.54x^2$$

where:

x = quarters
x =0, January 1985
$p \leq .1$

This equation clearly demonstrates that lotto games have been on the decrease throughout the period analyzed and that the lottery commission has not found a way to revive interest in these games.

Figure 6.5
Pennsylvania's Lotto Sales, 1985–1992

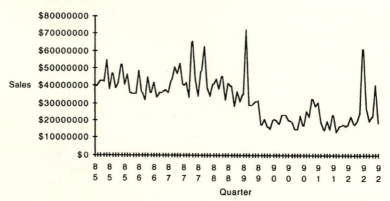

The equation that describes the trend for sales of Pennsylvania's daily number game (Figure 6.6) is the following:

$$Y(\text{sales}) = 70 + 7.06x - 0.03x^2$$

where:

x = quarters

x = 0, January 1985

$p \leq .03$

For practical purposes, this equation indicates that sales of Pennsylvania's daily number lottery are flat at about $70 million per quarter throughout the time period studied. There was a slight rise in sales at the beginning of the period studied and a slight decline in sales near the end of the period studied, but the overall trend is flat.

The preceding results are a cause for more than a bit of alarm not only for Pennsylvania's lottery officials but for members of both the executive and legislative branches of Pennsylvania's gov-

Figure 6.6
Pennsylvania's Daily Number Sales, 1985–1992

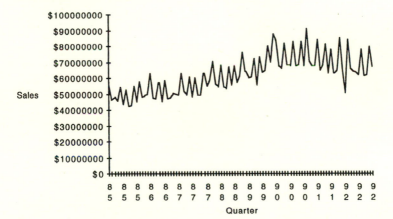

ernment. None of the three segments of Pennsylvania's lottery are capable of providing additional revenue for the state. In fact, sales of one of the segments (lotto games) have been falling for the past eight years, while another segment (instant games) also appears to be on the downside of its product life cycle. Perhaps the one bit of good news for lottery officials is that the game (daily numbers) on which they place their greatest hopes has at least been able to keep its sales steady, although even this appears to be in jeopardy. But clearly, Pennsylvania officials are becoming increasingly concerned over the lack of growth in lottery sales. While revenue from the lottery is at best steady, expenditures for the programs that the lottery is supporting are rising. How this deficit is to be covered is a major concern for both executive and legislative officials.

Strategic Options for New Gambling Initiatives in Pennsylvania

To close this deficit between the funds that the lottery raised and the amount that was spent providing services for Pennsylvania's elderly, Pennsylvania's public policy makers had three choices:

1. Reduce benefits to Pennsylvania's elderly,
2. Change the operating strategy of the lottery in order to obtain maximum benefits from the lottery, or
3. Seek new gambling initiatives in order to raise new revenue.

Obviously, the first option, which would reduce benefits to Pennsylvania's senior citizens, would pose a number of political difficulties. One measure that was taken to deal with falling lottery revenue was to freeze the Pennsylvania lottery's contribution to support public transportation for the elderly. But even this measure has encountered major difficulties. The freeze has caused the basic fares on most of Pennsylvania's local public transit to be among the highest in the United States. For example, the basic fare on Philadelphia's public transportation system is $1.50, compared with a basic fare of $0.85 in Boston. Since the elderly and very young are the primary users of public transit, these fares have been criticized as an "unfair" tax on the poor, and there have been calls for the state to use its general revenues to help reduce fares. Needless to say, Pennsylvania's legislators would prefer to be able to fund public transit in a more politically palatable manner. In other less populated parts of the state, this freeze in public transit support has caused severe cuts in service, even the threat of total cessation of service (*Scranton Times*, December 23, 1993, p. 1).

Hence, there is general consensus among Pennsylvania's public officials that gambling revenue has to be increased; otherwise, cuts in services to the elderly will have to be made. Once again, the disagreement will revolve around the amount of revenue that needs to be raised and how the revenue ought to be raised. Next, the internal and external forces that will influence the overall gambling strategy for Pennsylvania will be examined.

Internal Political Environment: Two Conflicting Views. Pennsylvania's Democratic governor Robert Casey was elected governor in 1986 and reelected in 1990. Throughout his entire tenure as governor, he has been a consistent opponent of expanded legalized gambling in any form or any place in Pennsylvania. He has also instructed the lottery commission to pursue a low-keyed advertising campaign and avoid advertisements that "glorify" the glories that players could receive if they play the lottery. Lottery ads in Pennsylvania either have emphasized that proceeds support senior citizens or have been of the "humorous" variety. But as the previous section has made amply clear, this passive strategy toward promoting the lottery has led to a gradual but pronounced decline in lottery sales.

Meanwhile, the Pennsylvania legislature is a divided force in state politics. The House is controlled by the Republicans, while the state Senate is controlled by the Democrats. But if there is one issue on which legislative leaders of both parties can agree, it is on the possibility of legalizing various gambling opportunities in order to raise additional revenue.

So, unlike Massachusetts, there is a split between the executive and legislative branches of government on the advisability of legalizing additional forms of gambling. But this split is not a result of political party disagreements. In fact, the forces in the legislature that are providing the most support for legalizing other forms of gambling are a group of Democratic state senators. While the majority of Republicans also support these additional gambling venues, they have become merely interested spectators in a long, drawn-out political battle over legalized gambling in Pennsylvania.

External Political Environment: Please Don't Cross the Delaware. In determining what gambling strategy Pennsylvania ought to establish, public policy makers need to take into account the strategies of competitors—namely, in this "industry," the availability of gambling opportunities in neighboring states. Certainly one of the most frequently used arguments by legislators to justify their support of gambling initiatives has two parts:

1. Ought not the citizens of our state be able to play those games that are available in neighboring states, giving our constituents the freedom to "choose"?

2. Why shouldn't our state get its share of the revenue from these gambling activities?

It is the same rationale that was used in the Massachusetts debate over the appropriate state policy toward gambling. Table 6.2 lists the various gambling opportunities available to Pennsylvania officials as well as those that are being proposed in these states. Once again, it will be instructive to examine this type of table from two different perspectives.

Examining Table 6.2 from the horizontal perspective, the state that has been the most aggressive in instituting an overall gambling strategy is New Jersey. Currently, New Jersey is either considering instituting or has been actively engaged in almost every gambling option except for OTB. The other state that also appears to find gambling as an appealing alternative for financing of government is New York. In fact, almost every state (except for West Virginia) that borders on Pennsylvania seems to have made a fairly serious effort to raise revenue through a concerted gambling policy.

Table 6.2
Pennsylvania's Gambling Options: What's Being Played and What's Being Proposed in Neighboring States

State	Casino	Jai alai	Keno	Lottery	OTB	Pari-mutuel	Video Poker
Delaware	*	--	--	X	X	X	*
Maryland	*	--	X	X	--	X	*
New Jersey	X	--	*	X	*	X	X
New York	*	--	*	X	X	X	*
Ohio	*	--	--	X	*	X	*
Pennsylvania	*	--	*	X	X	X	*
West Virginia	--	--	--	X	--	--	--

X = Already being played

-- = Not being played

* = Proposed

When Table 6.2 is examined from the vertical perspective, it is quite evident that the two options that have the most appeal as future sources of revenue for the state coffers are casino gambling and video poker. Presently, only New Jersey has legalized casino gambling and video poker machines. The success that New Jersey has had in raising money from its casino establishments in Atlantic City has certainly caused neighboring states to view this revenue in a rather envious manner. It is somewhat surprising that keno gambling has only invoked mild interest among these states. However, all of them are engaged in lottery operations and offtrack betting and pari-mutuel betting seems to be readily accepted by constituents of these states.

Hence, the external competitive environment in which Pennsylvania finds itself in seeking additional gambling revenue is quite fierce. However, the need to raise additional nontax revenue is also significant, and so the internal pressure to enter these new gambling initiatives will also be great. How Pennsylvania's public policy makers deal with these forces will be examined in the next section.

Pennsylvania's Gambling Options: Keno, Casino Gambling, and Video Poker

The three types of gambling initiatives that were considered or proposed by legislators in 1993 were keno, casino gambling, and video poker. Once again, it should be pointed out that none of these proposals were backed by the governor of Pennsylvania or his staff. This, of course, makes a profound difference in the amount and type of legislative support needed to enact these proposals over a governor's veto. Still, it ought to provide the reader with some interesting insights into the rationales used by legislative leaders to further the state's commitment to gambling revenue and how they hope to position themselves when opportunities arise in the future to enact gambling initiatives.

Keno. Currently, the only state that borders on Pennsylvania that has keno gambling is Maryland. The other state that has shown interest in keno operations is New York. State senators from the areas that border Maryland have expressed the greatest interest in Pennsylvania's adoption of this form of gambling.

But the proposal for keno gambling never received any support from any legislative committee and appears temporarily to be a lost cause. There are two reasons for the demise of the keno proposal. First, the executive branch under Governor Casey's leadership was adamantly opposed to keno gambling. Since keno is placed in supermarkets, small food stores, or other sites where lottery tickets are currently sold, the governor argued that it is a form of gambling that preys on the poor. He had concerns that money that was intended to be spent on food would instead be used to buy keno tickets. Second, the Pennsylvania lottery commission argued against instituting keno gambling even if it would have been given control of the game. The Pennsylvania lottery commissioner was well aware of the decline in lottery sales that Maryland experienced when it started its keno game. The lottery commissioner also argued that keno gambling would require much more policing of gaming establishments in order to ensure that the game was being operated properly. In Pennsylvania, this is a particularly sensitive issue, given the previous scandal with the daily number lottery. Hence, the critics of keno won this round of the battle over keno, although it appears that keno's fate as part of Pennsylvania's gambling initiatives will definitely depend on the long-run results of keno in its neighboring state Maryland.

Casino Gambling. The gambling possibility that has provoked the greatest interest both in Pennsylvania as well as in other neighboring states is casino gambling. There are two areas where it has been proposed that casino gambling be established in Pennsylvania—in the Pocono resort areas and on the Philadelphia waterfront. The proposed casinos were to be operated by private corporations following the model that New Jersey had set up in allowing casino gambling in Atlantic City.

The chief advocate for casino gambling was state Senator Vincent Fumo of South Philadelphia, whose district includes a large section of the Philadelphia waterfront, in particular, the part of the waterfront from which riverboat gambling would be "launched." Senator Fumo is also the president of the state Senate, so his sponsorship of casino gambling was taken quite seriously. Fumo's arguments in favor of casino gambling were fairly standard but with a slight twist. In the spring of 1993, Philadelphia opened a new convention center that—it was hoped—would make Philadelphia a much more attractive convention site. At present, there are express trains from downtown Philadelphia to the casinos in Atlantic City to provide entertainment for the conventioneers. The trip takes approximately one hour. Senator Fumo argued that these conventioneers ought to be able to gamble in Philadelphia and thus avoid the hour trip to Atlantic City and at the same time, of course, spend their money in Philadelphia. Fumo also argued that waterfront casino gambling would make the convention center more attractive.

To garner additional support for his proposal, Fumo also wanted to legalize casino gambling in Pennsylvania's other tourist center, namely, the Pocono Mountains region. State senators from this region were quite enthusiastic about this proposal, particularly because the New York state legislature had a proposal to legalize casino gambling in the Catskill resort region. Hence, many Pennsylvania state senators argued that the best defense is an offense when it came to state gambling policy. Casino gambling would deny New Jersey some of its Pennsylvania customers while possibly attracting New York residents to casino gambling in a mountain setting.

However, Governor Casey opposed casino gambling, recalling that casino gambling has not benefited Atlantic City, that it is merely a regressive tax on the poor. In June 1993, Governor Casey became quite ill, eventually requiring a heart and liver transplant. During his recuperation from the transplant operations, he handed over the powers of the governor to Lieutenant Governor Mark Singel. In a bit of irony, acting Governor Singel was reported as saying that he would sign any bill that authorized casino gambling. However, Governor Casey issued a statement from his University of Pittsburgh hospital room stating that if forced he would return to Harrisburg (Pennsylvania's state capital) in order to veto any casino gambling measure. While Senator Fumo had enough support to pass a casino gambling measure, he did not have enough support to receive the two-thirds support of the state Senate needed to override Governor Casey's veto.

Casino gambling had suffered a temporary defeat. But Senator Fumo's final remark concerning the issue of casino gambling was, "Pennsylvania will have casino gambling as soon as that Puritan is out of the governor's chair." Since Governor Casey leaves office in 1995, it will be interesting to see if Senator Fumo's prediction comes true. It certainly appears that Bally Manufacturing, one of the largest casino operators in the United States, is betting on Senator Fumo. Recently, Bally bought a thirty-one-acre site along the river in South Philadelphia in anticipation of riverboat casino gambling (*Philadelphia Inquirer*, January 5, 1994, p. 1).

Video Poker. New Jersey, which is the lone state in the Mid-Atlantic region that permits video poker machines, has confined these games to its casino gambling facilities. It appears that in this region of the country video poker machines are tied to the establishment of casino gambling. In the New England region, video poker games were permitted to be operated in bars and restaurants and were not tied to the casino gambling question.

In Pennsylvania, the establishment of video poker machines was tied to the casino gambling issue. Presently, there are bars and restaurants in Pennsylvania that are permitted to operate video poker machines, but there are no cash prizes associated with winning on these machines. While Massachusetts lawmakers wanted to use video poker games as a prop for the sagging fortunes of its taverns and bar owners, Pennsylvania's public policy makers seem to want to keep the gambling and alcohol issues separated, although obviously casinos would be permitted to serve alcohol. Thus, when the casino gambling initiative was defeated, any chance of video poker games was also defeated. It will be interesting to see if in the future the casino gambling issue will be "decoupled" from the video poker issue, especially if Pennsylvania's tavern, bar, and restaurant owners start agitating for video poker machines.

Conclusion

In some ways, this case analysis of Pennsylvania's struggle over state gambling policy is much more typical of what occurs in other states than the scenario in Massachusetts. The split in Pennsylvania's government between the executive and legislative branches over the advisability of introducing additional gambling initiatives is a classic confrontation that has occurred in many states. This confrontational start of additional gambling opportunities mimics the beginning of most of the lotteries in the United States. Initial efforts to start lotteries were thwarted by governors and antigambling forces who did not want the state to become involved in what critics considered to be addictive activities. However, the public generally sided with the prolottery forces, contending that citizens ought to be given a choice of whether or not they should gamble. Finally, given the public sentiment, when legislators had to choose between higher taxes or instituting a lottery, legislative leaders usually were able to muster enough votes to override any remaining gubernatorial objections. Of course, there have been candidates for governors who were elected on a platform that they would support a lottery proposal. This was certainly the case in the latest Texas gubernatorial race. So it is interesting to note that these additional gambling initiatives are meeting with the same type of resistance that the lottery met when it was first proposed.

If history is a good predictor, then these additional gambling initiatives will eventually be passed, overcoming any initial opposition. It certainly appears to be the case in Pennsylvania, where Senator Fumo's comment about waiting out the present governor's opposition in order to enact casino gambling in the near future appears to be playing out the way Senator Fumo predicted. Most of the announced candidates (including the present lieutenant governor) for Pennsylvania's gubernatorial race in 1994 have indicated that they will support any casino gambling initiative put before them.

The Pennsylvania case also points out that casino gambling has become an acceptable form of gambling that will not only be tolerated by public policy officials but whose enactment seems to be welcomed by government officials who view it as a revenue windfall for their states. Just as states have been competing with each other for years to attract industry to their states, casino gambling now appears to have become a symbol of a state's commitment to attract tourist dollars. Public officials view tourists as a source of income that can be secured without raising taxes on the voters who elect them, even if casino gambling is the vehicle.

SUMMARY

In comparing and contrasting the experiences of Massachusetts and Pennsylvania in regard to the expansion of gambling, the similarities and dissimilarities between the two states' political and economic policy processes are striking. The internal environment that policy makers faced over the gambling issue had both an economic and political component. Meanwhile, the external environments that each state faced as it formulated an overall gambling strategy were remarkably similar. The final two sections of this summary will summarize the similarities between the Massachusetts and Pennsylvania policy processes as they face the issue of increasing state-sponsored gambling opportunities.

Internal Environment

In contrasting the internal environments of Massachusetts and Pennsylvania, one cannot help but notice the economic and political differences that in large measure account for the different internal environments that confronted public policy makers from each state. In evaluating the economics of gambling for each state, most observers would maintain that the Massachusetts lottery is much more successful than Pennsylvania's lottery for two reasons: First, the Massachusetts lottery has consistently achieved a higher per capita rate of revenue for the state; second, it would appear that the Massachusetts lottery provides a much more solid basis for further growth in lottery revenues. Therefore, one would surmise that the Massachusetts lottery commissioner would be making a case to preserve the status quo, while the Pennsylvania lottery commissioner would be advocating additional gambling opportunities in order to supplement falling lottery revenues. Obviously, the scenario that actually occurred was the exact opposite one would have imagined, given the economic evidence.

The reason for this rather surprising economic scenario is, of course, the internal political environment that was played out in each of these states. Again, this result is somewhat unexpected. Given that the Massachusetts governor's office is occupied by a Republican and that both houses of the Massachusetts legislature are controlled by the Democrats, one might have expected major political battles over the "morality" of additional gambling issues. But, in fact, the controversy over gambling was waged over what games ought to be instituted and who would control the revenue that would come from these additional gambling ventures. The morality of additional gambling initiatives was never really an issue in Massachusetts. Meanwhile, in Pennsylvania, the governorship and the state Senate were both controlled by Democrats; so one would have thought that these two stakeholders would have provided a uniform point of view on additional gambling initiatives, particularly in light of falling lottery revenues. Instead, we witnessed how the Democrats held quite diverse opinions about the advisability of starting new state-sponsored gambling initiatives. A majority of the Democratic legislators, along with their Republican colleagues, were quite willing to permit additional gambling opportunities, especially casino gambling. Governor Casey and other "traditional" Democrats constituted the primary force opposing adoption of casino gambling.

In both Massachusetts and Pennsylvania, it is generally acknowledged that the lottery is no longer capable of generating enough revenue to fund the various good causes for which it was instituted. Because of this shortfall in revenue, other gambling options have become politically acceptable for both Democrats and Republicans. In reality, the only political forces able to delay the eventual implementation of additional gambling opportunities are traditional Democrats such as Governor Robert Casey of Pennsylvania and Governor Mario Cuomo of New York. But as this breed of traditional Democrat turns over power to the new pragmatic Democrats, the future for almost universal availability of casino gambling seems assured.

External Environment

While the internal environments facing Massachusetts and Pennsylvania in regard to the expansion of gambling were quite different, the external environments (i.e., the states of New England and the Mid-Atlantic region) facing these two states are remarkably similar, at least in terms of expanding gambling opportunities. Both regions have weathered a severe economic downturn, and states in these regions have viewed the lottery and other forms of gambling as ways of raising revenue without adding any further burden to a state's economy or taxpayers. Public policy makers in both regions are well aware of the gambling initiatives of neighboring states and seem to be quite willing to compete with neighboring states in seeking gambling revenue. Throughout this chapter, one of the most powerful arguments used by advocates of expanding gambling opportunities to further their cause has been, Citizens of our state are gambling in other states, so why shouldn't this revenue be kept at home?

The other constant in examining the external gambling environment for both Massachusetts and Pennsylvania is the almost universal acceptance of casino gambling as the vehicle to expand gambling activities. Both the New England and Mid-Atlantic regions have one state that has casino gambling, and it has forced all of the other states in those regions to consider the possibility of casino gambling. While it might appear that most of the states are using a "follower" strategy in regard to casino gambling, in reality these states are considering casino gambling simply to retain their "market share" of the gambling revenue available to them. Since this revenue is considered "painless," state officials are quite loathe to surrender this revenue to any other state, especially if failure to legalize casino gambling or any other type of gambling activity would force a governor and a legislature to raise sales or income taxes.

This general acceptance of casino gambling by most states widens the scope of gambling in two significant ways. First, the decision to legalize casino gambling presents states with a whole host of new difficulties. In many ways, it is the start of a "fourth wave" of gambling. In Chapter 1, it was asserted that one of the aspects that has made the present third wave of gambling unique is its reliance on state ownership. Almost all of the lotteries that have been instituted since 1964 have been operated by the state. But with the advent of casino gambling, a different phenomenon is rapidly spreading throughout the United States, namely, licensing gambling opportunities to private firms, or what has been termed the *privatization* of gambling. This phenomenon of privatization is actually a return to the traditional manner of conducting gambling in the United States used during the first two waves of lottery activity. Chapter 7 will present a model that will attempt to define what a "successful" privatization of gambling might require of both the state and the private gambling entrepreneur.

The widespread acceptance of casino gambling will also have an impact on any future strategy that a state might want to develop, especially in terms of maintaining its own state-operated lottery. In the final chapter, there will be a discussion of how the lottery segment of the gambling industry might adapt itself to the rapidly changing gambling industry. Finally, a series of likely scenarios about the future of gambling will be presented along with a commentary about what the lottery and gambling phenomena have to tell us about the present state of public policy making in the United States.

PART III

THE FUTURE OF LOTTERIES AND LEGALIZED GAMBLING

Chapter 7

Privatization and
Other Strategic Issues
Concerning the
Regulation of Gambling

One of the more interesting developments in state-sponsored gambling has been the subcontracting of lottery games to private corporations such as G-Tech and Scientific Games. When states subcontract—also termed *privatize*—states permit a private firm to conduct the lottery, and the state merely takes a certain percentage (usually 2 to 4 percent) of either the gross amount in the betting pool (as in pari-mutuel betting) or a certain percentage of net revenue (varying from 5 to 8 percent). The first state to privatize its lottery was South Dakota.

When three states recently (Georgia, Nebraska, and Texas) began a lottery, they auctioned off the right to run their lottery to either G-Tech or Scientific Games. Since these firms manufacture most of the instant game tickets, which is the game of preference for new lotteries, given the Massachusetts experience, it makes sense to let these firms operate a state's initial lottery offerings. These states, then, proceeded to set up "gambling commissions," which have the task of overseeing the operations of the lottery, racing (all forms), and nonprofit gaming such as bingo. Until this trend started, lotteries had been set up and solely operated by state agencies. Hence, the questions that this chapter addresses are:

1. What are the motives behind the privatization of gambling by government?
2. What are the possible consequences of this privatization of gambling
   by the states?

To provide answers to these questions, a framework will be provided to evaluate the privatization process, and then this framework will be used to determine the possible positive and negative
consequences of a privatization of state-sponsored gambling.

A FRAMEWORK FOR EVALUATING PRIVATIZATION

A government's policy decision to privatize a firm that has been
traditionally nationalized is usually evaluated in terms of whether
or not economic efficiency has been increased in either the short
run or the long run. If the privatization has increased economic
efficiency, then it is proclaimed a success (Vickers and Yarrow,
1988). In the case of privatizing state gambling operations, efficiency would seem to imply that the state would increase its revenue by handing over the operations of the lottery rather than
continuing to operate the lottery by itself.

But in the case of privatization of gambling, this preoccupation
with economic efficiency fails to measure the political consequences that any decision to privatize might have (Savas, 1987, p.
233). To deal with this deficiency, Pint (1990, pp. 267–270) has
proposed using a "rational-choice" framework that is "based on
the view that interest group members and politicians act as ratio-
nal decision-makers." It is essentially a cost-benefit analysis that
measures both the economic and political consequences for every
interest group or stakeholder that will be affected by a proposed
privatization. Hence, the real question becomes how to develop a
calculus that would enable a researcher to calculate the economic
and political consequences of a proposed privatization for every
interested group.

This would seem to be a daunting task. For even if there could
be agreement on what constituted the costs and benefits of any pri-

vatization for every stakeholder, these calculations could only be determined for short-run costs and benefits and would be nearly impossible to estimate for the long run. However, this distinction between short-run and long-run costs and benefits provides an opportunity to develop a framework that utilizes both Vicker and Yarrow's emphasis on efficiency and Pint's observation that political consequences must be taken into account in determining the success of any privatization policy by government (McAllister and Studlar, 1989, table 8). This measurement of economic and political consequences was one that policy makers had to make when they initially started a lottery, and now it seems they will have to continue this evaluation as they decide whether or not it is in a state's best interest to turn over the control of a lottery to a private concern.

The Framework

The purpose of this framework (shown in Figure 7.1) is to provide the reader with a four-step process by which a privatization of gambling (or any privatization of a traditional service provided by the state such as water, sewerage, etc.) can be evaluated. The rest of this section will be used to explain how this process works. Our discussion will begin with an examination of the short-run economic and political criteria that will be employed in this framework.

Cell 1 of the framework or matrix is concerned with the efficiency that the newly privatized firm displays in the period immediately after privatization. The questions that need to be asked are: Has privatization enabled the firm to develop business strategies that lead to increases in market share and/or profits? (It should be noted here that the business strategy of the firm might be to sacrifice short-term profits in order to obtain increases in market share that hopefully will lead to increases in long-term profitability. Hence, the goal of a newly privatized firm could be either to achieve increases in market share or to increase profitability, although obviously these two goals do not have to be mutually exclusive.) Is the newly privatized firm better able to achieve oper-

Figure 7.1
A Framework for Evaluating the Privatization Process

	Short Run Consequences	Long Run Consequences
Economic	Business Efficiency Increases; More Revenue [1]	Corporate Options Increase; Diversification [3]
Political	Gains by Various Stakeholder Groups [2]	Stakeholders' Options Increase [4]

ating economies and to reduce its overall cost structure? It is this cell that has been the primary focus of economists such as Vicker and Yarrow. The reason for this is obvious: If privatization is not successful in economic terms in the short run, then it can have little hope of being successful in the long run either economically or politically. This cell is also by far the easiest to measure using available data. Hence, it is the one most evaluators of a privatization process have utilized.

But it is rather naive to postulate that economic efficiency is the only short-run goal to be analyzed during the privatization process. There is also a need for political efficiency in the short run, which is represented by cell 2. While many political processes are repre-

sented as zero-sum games, the privatization process is certainly
not one of them. As Pint (1990, p. 268) has pointed out, the privatization process is quite inefficient if the process does not benefit
most of the stakeholders who take part in the process, since this
could lead to a situation where the privatization process is too easily reversed. Hence, to ensure that the privatization process is efficient, the majority of stakeholders in the privatization process
must benefit directly from any privatization. Government must
obtain more revenue (or cut its losses in terms of reduced subsi-
dies) from the newly privatized firm. Customers must benefit
either by receiving a better-quality product/service or by paying
less for the goods/services that the firm provides. Finally, other
interested stakeholders, such as public interest groups and local
government, must be satisfied that their interests will not be dis-
counted when short-term policy decisions are being made for the
newly privatized firm.

Cell 3 represents the long-run economic interests of privatization and has as its goal the development of a corporate strategy that
will ensure the continued profitability of the newly created privatized firm. The development of this corporate strategy demands
that the privatization process provides the firm with new options in
planning its future strategies. Can the firm pursue a diversification
strategy so that the firm is no longer dependent on just one source
of revenue? Has privatization enabled the firm to compete in new
markets outside those traditionally present? Should the newly privatized firm become vertically integrated either forward or back-
ward? Also, the type of management that is needed to make
decisions of this type is not usually found in nationalized or highly
regulated firms. This is particularly true in the case of gambling. It
would also seem that in order for the privatized firm to engage in
this sort of long-term corporate strategy thinking, new managers
as well as a new corporate culture would have to be developed.

Obviously, if the privatized firm is going to choose any of these
corporate strategies, then it must be given the freedom by government to do so. The amount of freedom that the government can
give to a privatized enterprise is precisely the issue that cell 4 has

as its chief concern. Just as the privatized firm needed to have options in order to establish a basis for long-term economic efficiency, the other stakeholders, which were mentioned in the previous discussion about short-term political efficiency, also need to retain some measure of power/influence over the future course of any previously nationalized firm. For if the privatization process is to be politically viable in the long run, then government must decide the amount of power it will exercise in order to satisfy all of the constituencies to which the firm is responsible.

In summary, this framework for evaluating the privatization process requires the evaluator to ask a series of questions about the economic and political effects that the privatization of a firm will have both in the short run and in the long run. In the short run, the newly privatized firm not only has to be a modest success economically but also needs to satisfy the vast majority of stakeholders, who must perceive that privatization has worked for their betterment. The criterion for the long-run success of a privatization is the development of various options for all of the stakeholders in the process. For the firm, this involves having the ability to implement a new corporate strategy for itself. Meanwhile, government as well as other stakeholders must maintain a measure of influence over how goals will be set by the privatized firm. The unique feature of this framework is that it recognizes not only the trade-offs that the evaluator must make between the short- and long-run objectives of privatization but, most important, the trade-offs between the economic and political goals of privatization. For some observers, nationalization represents the subjugation of economic objectives to political objectives, while privatization can be perceived as the triumph of the economic goal of efficiency over political concerns of equality. What this framework is trying to point out is that a privatization cannot be evaluated correctly unless proper attention is paid to both the economic and political compromises that must be made if the privatization is to take place successfully.

The rest of this chapter will be spent examining a very controversial but unique privatization process: the privatization of state-sponsored gambling.

EVALUATING THE PRIVATIZATION OF STATE-SPONSORED GAMBLING

Cell 1

This is the cell that emphasizes economic efficiency in the short run. A success in this cell is measured by how fast a private firm can increase revenue for the state from gaming operations. But why would a privatized lottery be in a better position to increase revenue than one operated by the state? To increase revenue, a privatized gambling concern would need either to increase sales or to cut costs in comparison to the state-operated lottery. How would this privatized lottery achieve either or both of these goals in order to increase overall revenue?

To increase sales, a privatized lottery would be able to advertise in a much more aggressive manner than state-controlled lotteries normally are permitted. For example, the Massachusetts state lottery advertising budget was limited to $2 million a year. In many other states, the amount of advertising permitted is limited to some percentage of net revenue, usually 2 to 3 percent. However, a privatized gambling firm would not have to limit its advertising budget. The other advantage that would accrue to a privatized gambling concern would be lack of a limit on the type of advertising that could be employed. To avoid controversy, most state lotteries use fairly "tame," general advertising, trying to show how "fun" it is to play a lottery game. A privatized lottery could be much more aggressive in advertising. Rather than generalized advertising, advertising could be used to target certain niche markets as well as displaying the "dream" of winning lottery millions in much more graphic terms.

Besides more aggressive advertising, a privatized lottery could also employ a much more aggressive sales force. Presently, most state lottery salespersons are salaried employees. A privatized firm would be much more inclined to employ commissions as the basis for its sales force. Another area where a privatized firm could expand sales opportunities is making additional outlets available for lottery tickets available. Perhaps a privatized lottery could also increase the prizes (presently 1 percent) given to vendors as a reward for aggressively "hawking" lottery tickets.

One area where a privatized firm would have a distinct advantage over the state-controlled lottery games is in the area of cutting costs. Since state employees are protected by civil service regulations as well as having more costly fringe benefits, the cost of operating a private lottery ought to be substantially lower than a state-operated lottery. Another cost "benefit" derived from privatizing lottery operations would be the more liberal use of part-time employees as opposed to unionized state employees. These arguments are generally used in support of any privatization process; that is, a private concern ought to be able to provide the good or service at a cheaper (more efficient) rate than a state-controlled operation.

The case for privatizing state-sponsored gambling rests on the ability of the private concern to expand the lottery's markets as well as to reduce the costs of operating the lottery. In the next cell, the political ramifications of privatization will be analyzed.

Cell 2

The short-run political consequences of privatizing lottery operations are centered around the issue of whether or not this privatization is considered "fair." Trying to define what one means by *fair* is, of course, a daunting and thankless task. However, in the context of privatization, it is generally centered around the issue of whether the majority of stakeholders (groups interested in an issue) are "better off." The four major stakeholders in the gambling arena are government, customers, unions, and antigambling interest groups. Hence, the emphasis in this cell is no longer on economic or revenue issues but rather on how the political process deals with the interests of groups that are concerned with gambling.

Government officials, whether they are from the executive or the legislative branches of government, have borne criticism from many antigambling groups. As we have seen, this criticism is centered around two issues: (1) The state should not be in a business that is potentially addictive; (2) the payoff of lottery games is not fair—that is, a greater percentage ought to be given back to the bettors. By privatizing a lottery, state officials avoid both of these criticisms. Government officials simply point out to these groups that they are no longer in the gambling business, and they have no wish to "legislate morality." However, the government will take its portion of the profits at absolutely no risk to government. It allows government officials to broadcast their belief in an individual's ability to "choose" while showing voters how efficient government can be. It cerainly appears that the privatization of lottery games is an ideal short-run solution for elected officials.

Meanwhile, the customers of lottery games potentially benefit from privatizing lottery games in two ways. First, a private firm is much more likely to provide a broader array of games. Second, a private lottery firm would be much more likely to increase the percentage of winners for lottery games. Currently, these percentages are fixed by lottery commissions. But a private lottery firm could use increases in payoffs to generate more interest in playing games since its costs would be lower than those of a state-controlled lottery. The role of the lottery commission would be to ensure the public that the games are fair (in this context, no fraud). Hence, the customers could potentially enjoy greater variety and better payoffs under a privatized lottery.

The unions that represent state lottery workers are in a "no-win" situation. Obviously, they would like to oppose the privatization of the lottery since it will most likely result in the loss of union jobs. However, the amount of sympathy that state lottery workers could mobilize does not appear to be overwhelming. Certainly, the firm that is initiating the privatization of a lottery will offer to keep current lottery workers but without state benefits. Also, the current trend toward the privatization of state services will not help these workers, given the fact that the lottery does not provide a necessary good or service. The argument could also be made, since the lottery is a form of entertainment, why should the workers providing this entertainment be protected from the forces of the marketplace.

Interest groups that are leading antigambling campaigns are also in a rather curious political position. Certainly, a common complaint among these groups is that the state ought not to be in the gambling business. So one would think that these groups would be rejoicing over the privatization of gambling since it removes the state from the gambling business. However, these groups realize that they would have a much greater influence over a state lottery commission than they would over a private firm operating lottery games for the state. The amount of political pressure that could be applied to a successful private firm is minimal as long as the gambling activity has been sanctioned by the state. This is not the case with a state-controlled lottery, which has to answer directly to legislative committees that are much more susceptible to public pressures and negative news accounts of gambling activities. For these antigambling interest groups, privatization can be claimed as a victory insofar that it removes the state as the chief sponsor of gambling activities, but in reality, it actually weakens the influence that these groups have over the future course of gambling activities.

Cell 3

One of the key assumptions that supporters make about gambling is its long-term viability as a revenue source for government. In Chapter 4, we saw that the only lottery game that seemed capable of providing long-term growth in revenues was the instant game. However, the rate of growth did not even begin to satisfy the ever-increasing demands by government officials for more revenue. Even Massachusetts, which has used instant games to their maximum advantage, seems willing to sacrifice this success to venture into new gambling arenas. Hence, it certainly appears that the goal of many state governments is to increase gambling revenue, and the strategy that most states are willing to undertake to achieve this goal is diversification, that is, legalize many more forms of gambling. So the question becomes: What is the best "structure" to implement this new gambling strategy?

Alfred Chandler's famous dictum "Structure follows strategy" seems to apply to this situation (Chandler, 1962). As states expand · gambling opportunities to their constituents, it would certainly appear that a new structure to oversee these gambling enterprises is needed. The lottery commissions that are operating lottery games contain neither enough staff nor the expertise to simultaneously operate keno, OTB, video poker, and casino gambling operations. To make sure that these new gambling ventures bring in the maximum amount of revenue to the state, gambling operations must be coordinated.

There are two possible solutions. The state could set up an overall gaming agency that would operate all forms of gambling in the state. Obviously, this solution would require the state to hire many more employees, to buy gaming equipment, to build video poker locations as well as casinos, and to maintain these machines and casino sites. To choose this solution, the state needs to make a fairly heavy capital investment.

The other answer to this structure question is, of course, to privatize these new gambling operations. This solution offers many advantages to the state. First, the cost of buying and maintaining new gaming equipment would be borne by the private operators. Second, the risk of failure also rests solely with the private operators. Finally, the state gets its cut of the funds at absolutely no risk to the state. In many ways, the privatization of other forms of gambling would resemble pari-mutuel betting on horse racing. In states where pari-mutuel betting is permitted, these states set up a state racing commission whose salaries are paid by the individual owners of the track. The state takes a certain percentage of the betting pool and is assured of revenue. Obviously, if private operators run video poker parlors and full-scale casinos, a similar regulatory setup could, and probably would, take place.

In summary, by pursuing gambling as a source of revenue, the state is implicitly sanctioning a long-run strategy of diversification, that is, legalizing various forms of gambling. But for the state to involve itself in these operations, it would need to make a huge investment in both equipment and buildings as well as personnel.

So it would appear that privatization of gambling is the state's best chance of fulfilling the dream of risk-free revenue from its constituents.

Cell 4

Politically, the privatization of gambling in the long run offers both the executive and legislative branches many advantages. Obviously, the governor can request, and the legislature can approve (or as is the case in many states, the legislature approves over the governor's veto), whatever additional gambling is thought appropriate. But privatization also has another political advantage: By taking the operations of gambling out of various state commissions, it also puts to rest "infighting" over who controls the funds as well as the operations that come from gambling activities. In Chapter 6, we witnessed how this infighting was precisely the central issue that the Massachusetts legislature had to deal with as it decided how much it was going to expand its gambling opportunities in the state.

Another long-run stakeholder in the privatization of gambling is the customer. Privatization offers the customer two advantages in the long run. First, by removing the state from its monopoly position in the gambling arena, the customer should benefit from the competition that will develop to entice gamblers into their various games. One can foresee alliances made between hotel owners and restaurants to attract gamblers to their establishments. Gambling will become another element in an entertainment package.

The other stakeholders in the long-run privatization of gambling are antigambling groups such as Gamblers Anonymous as well as various church and civic organizations. By removing the state as the only beneficiary of gambling activity, these groups will now be able to dismiss the "good" cause that lotteries and other gambling can be said to support. The fight against legalized gambling will be moved to the legislative committees and the governor's office. It is easy to imagine that these groups will probably move to have gambling profits taxed at a higher rate than other corporate profits or to have a set percentage of their profits set aside for programs that deal with individuals who are addicted to gambling. In many ways, the privatization of gambling clarifies who the "enemy" is, and this is quite important for groups that wish to renew the public's interest in an issue such as gambling.

CONCLUSION

Privatization of state-operated lottery games at first sounds like an unlikely idea. After all, why should the state share its gambling revenue with a private corporation or firm? However, as the state seeks to expand its gambling horizon, the amount of money invested and risk taken increase substantially. Politically, the number of stakeholders who could benefit potentially from the privatization of gambling also increases dramatically.

As we saw earlier, gambling as a form of entertainment must be tolerated. By privatizing gambling activities, it appears that this tolerance level is increased. Gambling appears to be a prime example of what ethicists term the "slippery slope" argument—that is, if one permits even the smallest opening, then the floodgates are eventually opened. In many ways, the privatization of gambling is the logical conclusion to the ethical dilemma that gambling poses. Once a state-sponsored lottery (the small opening) is permitted to support a good cause, it does seem only a matter of time until there will be calls for legalizing all types of gambling in the private sector (floodgate) in order to support all kinds of state activities. Indeed, the privatization of gambling does appear to be the future of gambling in this country. However, the final chapter examines the other possible solutions to the gambling crisis.

Chapter 8

Concluding Remarks on Lotteries and Gambling

The purpose of this book was to examine the interactions of public policy makers with the business of operating state-sponsored lotteries. The preceding chapters have shown that this task is a complex one that requires analyzing not only the various rationales used by public policy makers to justify these activities but also the strategies that lottery commissioners need to employ to ensure that the lottery can fulfill the revenue expectations of those same legislators. The objective of this concluding chapter is to discuss the viability of the gambling industry in the future. It is only one of many industries whose existence has to be sanctioned by public policy makers. While certainly some of the issues facing the gambling industry are unique, there are clearly some implications for other highly regulated industries—such as alcohol, oil, and chemical—that are a source of direct revenue for government.

To accomplish this task, this chapter will be divided into three parts. In the first part, the empirical results from Chapters 4 and 5 as well as the case studies in Chapter 6 will be reviewed to determine the current state of the lottery and gambling industry in the United States. The next section will present the various strategies that states could employ as they try to predict their future in the gambling industry and its implications in terms of future policy as well as its impact on revenue for these states. Finally, there will be a commentary on the implications that this "gambling revolution" has had and will have on the present and future conduct of public policy.

A BRIEF SUMMARY OF THE CURRENT STRATEGIES FOR STATE-SPONSORED GAMBLING

In Chapter 4, the various strategies that states have employed in initiating a lottery were discussed. For states that started their lotteries in the 1970s, the initial game of preference was the daily number. Since the daily number was a well-established street game, these state lotteries were merely legalizing an activity that had existed for years. This strategy was particularly successful in large urban areas—for example, the District of Columbia. Meanwhile, when states with large populations such as New York, Florida, and California entered the lottery business, they focused their marketing resources on lotto games. The rationale behind this "home run" strategy was that these large-population states would build very large jackpots that would promote ever-increasing interest in these lotto games. Recently, when states such as Minnesota, Iowa, and Georgia started a lottery, the first game that was introduced was the instant game. To implement this instant game strategy, the lottery commissioner had to frequently introduce new games and renew "seasonal" interest in various types of instant games.

The driving force behind the adoption of all of these different types of lottery games was the product life cycle phenomenon that surrounds these lottery games. Like all forms of entertainment, these lottery games have to maintain the public's interest if they are going to be consistent revenue producers in the long run. The empirical results of Chapter 4 came to the following conclusions: (1) Only instant games were capable of any long-term sustained interest by players; (2) revenue from the daily number game could be kept constant; and (3) interest in lotto games cannot be sustained, and these games will die out. In addition, it was pointed out that even a successful instant game lottery strategy such as Massachusetts's would eventually be abandoned because it would not produce the amount of revenue that public officials were demanding as part of their "toleration" of a lottery. Hence, lottery officials throughout the United States were forced to diversify into all of the various types of gambling if revenues were to be maintained.

In Chapter 5, this diversification of state-sponsored gambling was analyzed. This expansion of gambling opportunities had various effects on lottery sales, depending on the gambling activity. Keno gambling as well as video lottery cannibalized existing lottery sales, although both of these gambling ventures increased overall gambling revenues for their respective states. There was no cannibalization of existing lottery sales with the introduction of other gambling options such as video poker, offtrack betting, and casino and riverboat gambling. However, there were other unforeseen side effects. For example, the move by the states into other forms of gambling such as video poker, keno, and offtrack betting has greatly reduced the ability of nonprofit organizations to use bingo and other charitable events to raise money. In general, it does appear that the public's appetite for gambling can still be expanded, although just how far it can be expanded has yet to be determined.

In Chapter 6, the experiences of Massachusetts and Pennsylvania with expanding gambling opportunities were examined in detail. Since Massachusetts has operated the most successful lottery in the United States, it would seem an ideal case to study. It would not be overstating the case to say that where Massachusetts goes with gambling, many states will try to follow. Pennsylvania was chosen since the dilemma that it faced in 1993 is one that seems to be plaguing many states: As lottery revenue either stabilizes or declines, how will the state fund the ever-increasing revenue needs of "good" causes that the lottery was supposed to fund?

In examining both the Massachusetts and Pennsylvania experiences, there were two criteria that had to be met before any further expansion of gambling opportunities would be approved. First, revenue from any new type of gambling had to be earmarked for a good cause that could attract widespread political support. This is critical in building the tolerance that legislators need to justify their support. Second, as the type of proposed legalized gambling becomes more "skilled" (i.e., in casino games such as blackjack and poker), strong support for private ownership or the privatization of gambling must develop. In Massachusetts, even with the support of both the governor and the legislature for various gambling initiatives, only keno gambling was adopted in 1993. For although there was general agreement about the need for more gambling revenue, the political leadership of Massachusetts could not agree on who would control this gambling revenue: the Republican governor or the Democratic legislature. Meanwhile, in Pennsylvania, there was a split between the executive and legislative branches of government over legalizing casino gambling in various parts of the state. This split was not over party affiliation but rather over the appropriateness of state-sponsored legalized gambling. The Democratic governor's opposition to casino gambling could not be overridden by the Democratic legislative supporters in 1993. Yet in both Massachusetts and Pennsylvania, it appears that casino gambling is almost a sure bet in the very near future.

This tendency of many states toward legalizing casino gambling or riverboat gambling also indicates another long-term trend, namely, the privatizing of gambling. It is significant that in both the Massachusetts and Pennsylvania cases the operators of any casino or riverboat gambling ventures were to be private entrepreneurs such as Bally's Inc., Donald Trump, and MGM Grand, and there was never any question about state-operated casinos. It is somewhat ironic that as the state legalizes more and more gambling opportunities, the amount of gambling activity that the state will actually operate itself will be much smaller. In Chapter 7, the criteria for a successful privatization of gambling were discussed, along with the various stakeholders who would need to be satisfied if this privatization was to be tolerated.

FUTURE OF GAMBLING IN THE UNITED STATES AND POSSIBLE STRATEGIES BY STATES

Critics of the current explosion in gambling activities such as I. Nelson Rose of the Whittier Law School in Los Angeles are quite bleak about the future of gambling in the United States. Rose is even so bold as to predict that all gambling will be "outlawed by 2029" (*New York Times*, August 29, 1993, p. E3). Rose's basis for making this prediction is historical. After all, gambling was outlawed after each previous wave of gambling activity. Hence, it will most certainly be outlawed this time. Debating whether or not history will repeat itself is certainly an interesting academic exercise. However, the pronounced differences between this third wave of gambling activity and the previous two waves certainly seem to negate the validity of this historical argument. Also, this debate is of little relevance to current public policy makers who need to balance state budgets by using gambling as a source of revenue. Certainly, all of the evidence in this study indicates that U.S. society will for the foreseeable future tolerate gambling as a legitimate form of entertainment as well as a source of revenue for the state. In fact, the gambling industry at present is one that is experiencing phenomenal overall growth, although segments of the industry such as the lottery appear to have reached their maximum growth potential.

The amount of growth that the gambling industry can achieve in the future will depend a great deal on the gambling strategy that the state employs to ensure continued play and support by the public. Hence, the survival of gambling is really in the hands of public policy makers and the private entrepreneurs they will employ to implement these policies and strategies.

There are basically three gambling strategies that public policy makers can formulate and implement. These strategies are not mutually exclusive (i.e., states will most likely use a combination of these strategies), but one of these strategies will form the basis on which other gambling ventures can be added. These strategies are (1) status quo, (2) expand and privatize, and (3) sweepstakes niche. The rest of this section will examine the implications of each of these strategic options.

Status Quo

Status quo is essentially an exit strategy out of the gambling industry by state officials. Certainly, lottery officials could maintain instant games, but the other two types of lottery games would eventually die out. What would happen to sales of instant games is also quite uncertain, especially if neighboring states pursued an aggressive gambling posture.

The advantage of this status quo strategy is that it is by far the least controversial of the three proposed strategies. Lottery games are considered benign forms of gambling that even the most fierce critics of state-sponsored gambling admit are essentially nonaddictive. Lottery games are certainly the most tolerated form of gambling and therefore the type that legislators find the most appealing.

However, the disadvantage of this type of gambling strategy is quite simply that legislators would need to find additional revenues to support the good causes that the lottery currently funds. In other words, if public policy makers in a given state elected to use this status quo strategy, there appears to be a heavy political price to be paid in the form of enacting new taxes.

Expand and Privatize

The goal of this strategy is to establish gambling as a consistent source of revenue for the state, and it is the one that most states seem to have chosen as their gambling strategy. To achieve this goal, it necessarily entails that new forms of gambling are established, since lottery games cannot maintain themselves, much less provide new revenue. Chapter 5 examined the effects that these additional forms of gambling—such as keno, video poker, OTB, video lottery, and casino and riverboat gambling—had on existing lottery games. Although some of these new gambling ventures did cannibalize existing lottery games, there was an overall increase in gambling revenue even when cannibalization of lottery games occurred (*Boston Globe*, August 22, 1993, p. 1).

Yet as we saw in Chapter 6, where we chronicled the events that led to Massachusetts's successful adoption of keno, the forces that were marshaled to support keno can be assembled in the future to support other gambling activities such as OTB, casino gambling, and riverboat gambling. It appears that the state legislatures cannot have enough of a good thing. In the search for more revenue, the sponsoring of more gambling opportunities for its citizens seems the easiest and least costly way (at least politically) of raising revenue.

But as the state legalizes more and more types of gambling, the questions of who should be operating these activities and what sorts of risk the state should be taking in sponsoring these gambling activities become interesting public policy questions. In Chapter 7, it was pointed out that the solution to both of these questions appears to be the privatization of gambling, especially casino and riverboat gambling. This solution seems to provide state legislatures with an ideal solution for two reasons: (1) It brings in a steady stream of revenue with no risk, and (2) it utilizes a process that has been warmly received by the public since it is viewed as one way of eliminating inefficient and costly government agencies. Private investors will open the OTB parlors and casinos, and the state will merely regulate their activities while using the state's share of wages for various good works.

While this scenario sounds reassuring, there are two problems that advocates of the privatization of gambling need to take into account. First, the historical argument against the future of gambling might have some basis if privatization is indeed the future of gambling in the United States. The history of private lotteries in the United States is quite disastrous, with the Louisiana lottery as the prime example of the corruption and greed associated with gambling operated for the state by private investors. It is hard to imagine how public officials would deal with the outcry against gambling once a private group was convicted of operating fixed gambling tables or slot machines. The easy solution to this problem for legislators would be to further regulate or abolish any form of gaming that seems to be prone to this sort of activity. Obviously, if there were a series of gambling scandals, then the public outcry would force the states to reconsider their legalized gambling activities.

The other problem with privatizing gambling is simply that it could be "too much of a good thing." Presently, Atlantic City and

Las Vegas are the two centers of legalized, privatized casino activity. But even with just these two sites operating in the United States, both are experiencing an "overcapacity" problem, with three Atlantic City casinos declaring bankruptcy. One must wonder just how profitable casino gambling would be if numerous other cities and states permitted casino gambling. For although the appetite for gambling seems to be endless, it is obviously a market that some say is already oversaturated.

It also should be pointed out that the casino gambling business seems to be changing drastically for two reasons. First, popularity of the various games is changing. In 1983, the amount of casino revenue that could be attributed to slot machine players was slightly over 25 percent. In 1993, almost 70 percent of all casino revenue came from the tingle and bells of the "slots." This drastic change in the preference of casino players for nontable games such as the slots and video poker has had a drastic effect on the operation of casino gambling. The amount of space given traditional table games such as blackjack, roulette, and craps has been drastically reduced to less than 30 percent of the space devoted to casino gambling. In other words, the typical casino player is no longer interested in the so-called skilled table games but wants the simple pleasure provided by pulling a slot machine. There are slot machines for every taste, ranging from $0.05-a-pull slots to $500-a-pull slots. Of course, the prizes and jackpots also range from $100 to those progressive slot machines that can pay prizes in the millions. But why would patrons continue to find casino gambling attractive if their local lottery commission could provide them such options as video lottery that could easily simulate the slot machine experience? The answer is that the "new" casino is one where the whole family can come (*Casino Player*, December 1993).

Besides this change in the games that attract casino players, there has been a change in the marketing of casino gambling. Las Vegas, which is still the capital of casino gambling, has recently experienced a total renewal of its image. The marketing strategy employed by Las Vegas today is that it can provide fun for the whole family—for example, a $475 million Treasure Island and the

$1 billion MGM Grand Hotel, which has an adjacent amusement park with seven rides and eight theme areas on thirty-three acres. To compete for the casino gambling dollar, casino operators will have to be able to attract the entire family. Hence, if a state decides to legalize casino gambling, it will need to provide its casino developers with a gimmick to attract families and conventioneers.

One thing that can be said safely is that future casinos will not be nearly as profitable as those that were operating alone in the early 1980s. The pot of gambling gold is proving to be much harder to grasp than most state legislators realize. However, despite these cautions, there can be little doubt that the privatization of gambling is sure to be a path that most states will follow in their search for additional "painless" revenue.

Sweepstakes Niche

A niche type of strategy that uses "sweepstakes games" as its primary gambling attraction has been employed quite successfully by European governments for many years. It differs from the typical state lottery in the United States in three respects: (1) The games are played much less frequently, usually coinciding with a major civil or religious holiday; (2) the prizes are much more substantial than those paid by U.S. state lotteries; and (3) the goal of these sweepstakes games is to fund a specific charity or cause.

This niche sweepstakes strategy would seem to respond to many of the critics of state-sponsored lotteries in the United States on a number of issues. Since these sweepstakes games would be played much less frequently, the addictive nature of gambling ought to be much less of a problem. Second, the proceeds of the sweepstakes games are designated well in advance to fund a specific charity, or good cause. No longer would the state have to be concerned with the product life cycle effect on its present lottery operations. Finally, lottery proceeds would no longer be going to the state treasury or be used to support education, health, or other uses that demand constant state attention. Hence, there would no longer be any need to constantly institute new types of lotteries or venture into other types of gambling to fund existing state responsibilities or to make further contributions to the state's treasury.

However, this sweepstakes concept would not prevent the current trend of privatization of gambling, especially casino gambling. But as was pointed out earlier, permitting this type of gambling is virtually risk free for the state. How successful the various casinos will be is quite questionable. Again, it would seem that the number of patrons and the amount of money that a casino would attract are limited and can only be divided in so many ways. Obviously, states could opt not to permit casino gambling. But the pressure that would be on state legislators to allow casino gambling appears to grow as neighboring states permit casinos to operate to attract patrons from outside their own states.

It would appear that the most viable strategy for states to adopt is this sweepstakes niche strategy along with privatization of other forms of gambling. However, this sweepstakes strategy cannot be adopted overnight and without some interesting political difficulties. Presently, several smaller lotteries are banding together in order to play a "super" lotto game known as "Powerball." The strategy behind this game is actually the same one being used by California, Florida, and New York—that is, hope that the weekly jackpots aren't hit so that the jackpots build up in order to raise more interest and attract more players. Obviously, these states have to give up a bit of their autonomy in joining this "lottery consortium" as well as dividing the jackpot along betting lines. The one negative development to the sweepstakes strategy is that it makes lottery revenue quite unpredictable and still doesn't solve the product life cycle question completely.

So *how* would this sweepstakes concept be instituted? A combination of federal and state cooperation would be needed. A national U.S. sweepstakes like the ones held in most European countries would certainly have no problem creating huge jackpot payoffs. Sweepstakes created for various good causes could be played once or even twice a year. Perhaps states in a particular region would be permitted to hold sweepstakes to support funding to recover from natural disasters such as hurricanes and floods.

This sweepstakes solution to the gambling problem contains more than a bit of irony. After the Civil War, the federal government banned states from sponsoring lotteries and essentially banned gambling throughout the United States. It now appears that the federal government will have to enter the lottery business to prevent states from being forced to compete with one another for every available gambling dollar. Just as the federal government forced state governments to enter the gambling business to fund programs in the less painful manner, now the federal government will most likely have to enter the gambling arena to establish some rationality to the gambling industry throughout the country.

How soon the federal government will enter the sweepstakes/lottery business is a bit difficult to forecast, but it would seem that the forces leading to this development are mounting. The first attempt at instituting a national sweepstakes was filed in Congress in 1989. The revenue from this sweepstakes game was to be used to reduce the federal deficit. While this measure never got out of committee, there have been several other attempts since 1989 to start a national sweepstakes, with each of these succeeding attempts gaining much more support. The most viable national sweepstakes proposal has been connected to the national health care issue, where proceeds from the sweepstakes would be used to fund basic medical research. It will be interesting to see what "good" cause is the eventual beneficiary of the first national sweepstakes. Of course, the effect that these national sweepstakes could have on state lottery games could be devastating to state finances. Hence, it would appear that the federal government will have to devise a way to share the proceeds of a national lottery with state governments to compensate them for the loss of lottery revenue. A new sort of revenue sharing appears to be coming to the states from the federal government.

CONCLUSION

Rose's prediction of gambling's demise by 2029 appears to be a bit premature. Admittedly, the future structure of the gambling industry will certainly be far different than it is today. The present gambling industry is dominated by state lottery games and an increasing number of states that have or will legalize casino and riverboat gambling. There has also been increased activity in keno, video poker, and OTB as well as sports gambling. There is little doubt that in the future casino gambling, legalized sports betting, OTB, and video poker will dominate the gambling industry, in both percentage of income and number of players. This change will take place for two reasons: First, the traditional lottery games will eventually die out, just as most brand names do. It is something that American marketers are currently experiencing even with brands that have commanded great loyalty from their customers, for example, Marlboro cigarettes (*The Economist*, September 7, 1991, p. 67). Second, the state's endless search for more revenue will doom the traditional lottery. It simply will not be able to provide the state with enough revenue; so the state will turn to other forms of gambling such as sweepstakes, casino gambling, OTB, and sports betting that can provide this revenue.

The strategy that the states will employ to achieve this new structure for the gambling industry will be privatization. The role of the state or government in general will change radically from owning and operating lotteries to regulating the various private gambling enterprises. This privatization strategy is one where the state takes no risk in operating these gambling establishments but will willingly take a rather substantial share of the gambling pot. Politically, this privatization of gambling allows the state to remove itself from the gambling arena. No longer can the critics of gambling accuse the state of fostering vice. The state merely is regulating and profiting from an activity that obviously the majority of Americans now approve. Hence, the economic and political consequences appear to be positive in both the short run and the long run. The criteria for a successful privatization that were given in Chapter 7 appear to be fulfilled and the stage set for a new era of legalized, privatized gambling.

However, the ties between privatization and gambling cannot be limited to just those that are economic and political. The social acceptability of gambling signals a shift in the morality by which

Americans sanction acceptable behavior. The rationale used by public policy makers to justify both of these trends (namely, gambling and privatization) in public policy has profound implications for the conduct of public policy in general. It is finally being acknowledged at all levels of American society. The following quote from *Time* is quite instructive:

If it is now acceptable for the whole family to come along to Las Vegas, that's because the values of America have changed, not those of Las Vegas. Deviancy really has been defined down. The new hang-loose all-American embrace of Las Vegas is either a sign that Americans have liberated themselves from troublesome old repressions and moralist hypocrisies, or else one more symptom of the decline of Western civilization. Or maybe both. (*Time*, January 10, 1994, p. 51)

In Chapter 3, it was shown that the rise of gambling activity corresponds to a rise in the ethics of tolerance. During the past thirty years, tolerance has become the highest civic virtue since it makes living in a pluralistic society possible. We have witnessed societies such as the former Soviet Union, China, Cuba, and Iran where there is no tolerance for any diversity. The preceding examples of conformist societies have convinced Americans that they certainly want to avoid this type of conformist ethic. It was in reaction to this conformist ethic that the ethics of tolerance was formulated. We should tolerate any action by an individual as long as that action enables that individual to be "true" to one's self and doesn't violate the self of another individual. This ethical principle represents the triumph of the self over all other moral considerations. Nor is this self the one that was advocated by Immanuel Kant, where the self is conceived as having to obey practical reasoning that can be used universally (Kant, 1964). Rather, the self that the ethics of tolerance promotes is the temporary self where long-term consequences are ignored so that the individual retains his or her autonomy. Just as American businesspersons have been criticized for focusing too much on short-term financial goals, it appears that U.S. public policy makers have also fallen into this trap of short termism. For this adoption of the ethics of tolerance, with its focus of tolerating activities in order to maintain the short-term peace, will have very interesting consequences for the type of society that the United States will be for the foreseeable future.

Unrestricted gambling has become morally acceptable (i.e., tolerated) in the United States only in association with the idea that there cannot be any society-wide objective moral norms. To tolerate other opinions or life-styles, morality has become a subjective preference, not an objective requirement; and the further we carry this line of reasoning, the more acceptable gambling becomes, since it is merely a subjective choice of the individual. Since the individual gambler is not hurting anyone else, then it is quite acceptable for the state to profit from this activity.

Furthermore, this connection between the privatization movement and the rise of gambling also coincides with the gradual diminution of concern that public policy makers have for the welfare and the rights of the lower classes and with a corresponding preoccupation that these same public policy makers have for preserving individual rights and a conception of the self. This new understanding of the goal of public policy results in the minimal state, and this minimal state has in turn spawned a conception of the self that is similarly minimal.

The continuing support that public policy makers give to gambling merely confirms the present U.S. cultural tendency to withdraw from public action into a cocoon of privacy. This preoccupation with the self or privacy poses some real challenges to the whole system of values and obligations that has historically been the basis of community and family life. Letting people be "free" to do what they want as long as they do not hurt others is hardly the type of ethic needed when U.S. society seems to be so desperately in need of a unifying communitarian spirit. Needless to say, this is not a call to subjugate the self or individual freedom totally under the banner of communitarian need. But certainly this study of the rise of gambling in the United States points out a real need for American society to develop an ethic that can be used to establish a series of objective norms that can be used to referee between the legitimate needs of society and the yearnings of the self.

Chapter 2 examines the scope of lottery activity throughout Europe, but one is particularly struck to the extent that lotteries have sprung up in eastern Europe and Russia. Needless to say, there is a bit of irony involved. Most of the countries have just emerged from a system of government where gambling was prohibited because Communist authorities maintained that there was no need for a bourgeois tactic such as a lottery to raise funds for social needs. The state would provide for the needs of workers and the poor. It was a system of government where the individual was totally subservient to the state, but in the end, it was a system that did not work.

It is also fascinating to witness how China has started to sponsor lottery games as it increasingly moves toward developing a market economy. It certainly appears that lotteries and legalized gambling are an integral part of any democratic system! Lotteries and gambling provide to these democratic governments the funds so that the state can take care of those who cannot take care of themselves.

But perhaps there is a positive side to the gambling craze that now infects almost every part of the world. Since taxpayers throughout the world seem to be joining their American counterparts in denouncing government spending, lotteries and legalized gambling seem to provide an outlet for individuals to show their concern about the plight of the unfortunate. Spain's massive lottery network certainly gives Spaniards a dual reason for playing the lottery: (1) a chance to become quite wealthy and (2) a chance to support a worthy cause. While critics of state-sponsored gambling have been especially critical of the advertising tactic of giving bettors unrealistic hopes of new-found riches, there could be a positive side to state-sponsored lotteries, sweepstakes, and gambling: The advertising needed to stroke an interest in these games will help to keep the plight of the unfortunate in the public eye. Given the proclivities of American society to isolate those segments of society that cause the majority to be uncomfortable, this possible role for gambling is quite worthy—even more so than the possible funds that gambling could raise for the poor and unfortunate of American society.

Indeed, gambling does appear to have become an integral part of American society and, for that matter, an integral part of most democracies throughout the world. Gambling is here to stay, although the current structure of state-controlled gambling will change, with most gambling activity gradually falling into private hands. The state will maintain control over such games as sweepstakes and establish regulatory power over legalized gaming operations. Whether or not the spread and acceptance of gambling as a form of entertainment will continue at its present rapid pace depends on the continued public acceptance of an ethic that places an absolute premium on the expression of the self over any claim for communitarian need. It is this glorification of the self that makes gambling not only a possibility but a necessity for the foreseeable future.

While the rise of lotteries and gambling has and will have many implications for American society as well as many other societies throughout the world, perhaps its greatest challenge to these societies is their need to restore a balance between the concerns of those who support the ethics of tolerance and those who support the ethics of sacrifice. The ability of a society to balance these moral viewpoints is the hallmark of a healthy and vibrant democratic system—a system that the world so desperately seeks as it is about to enter the twenty-first century.

Bibliography

Borg, Mary O., Paul M. Mason and Stephen L.Shapiro. *The Economic Consequences of State Lotteries.* Westport, CT: Praeger, 1991.

Boston Globe. Strahinich, John. "Mega-doubts," January 23, 1994, p. 67.

Boston Globe. Howe, Peter. "US Turns to Betting as Budget Fix," July 14, 1992, p. 25.

Boston Globe. Strahinich, John. "Sports Officials Oppose Weld on Legalized Betting," January 3, 1993, p. 16.

Boston Globe. Howe, Peter. "Indians Pursue a Golden Chance," August 22, 1993, pp. 58–59.

Boston Herald. Primack, Phil. "Weld and Gambling," January 3, 1993, p. 15.

Box, G.E.P. and G. C. Tiao, "Intervention Analysis with Applications to Economic and Environmental Problems," *Journal of the American Statistical Association* 70, 349 (March 1975): 70–79.

Casino Player. "More Slots," December 1993, pp. 8–12.

Chicago Tribune. "Cash Strapped Britain Pursues a Lottery for a Number of Reasons," December 23, 1992, pp. 34–35.

Chicago Tribune. "Spain's 'Fat One' Delivers Big," December 23, 1992, pp. 34–35.

Chandler, Alfred. *Strategy and Structure.* Cambridge, MA: MIT Press, 1962.

Clotfelter, Charles T., and Philip J. Cook. *Selling Hope: State Lotteries in America.* Cambridge, MA: Harvard University Press, 1989.

Crane, Robert Q. *The Lottery: A Reference Guide.* Braintree, MA: Massachusetts State Lottery Commission, 1989.

Daily Telegraph. "Going Dutch to Find a British Lottery," January 25, 1993, pp. 1–3.

DeBoer, Larry. "When Will State Lottery Sales Growth Slow?" *Growth and Change* 17 (January 1986): 29–35.

The Economist. "Gambling and Be Taxed," January 16, 1988, pp. 25–26.

The Economist. "Fading Brands," September 7, 1991, pp. 39–41.

The Economist. "Taking a Chance," December 21, 1991, p. 57.

The Economist, "Gambling and the State," April 17, 1992, pp. 67–68.

Les Echos. "FDJ Aims to Lift Turnover to 29 Billion in '92," September 24, 1992, p. 12.

Les Echos. "Societe de: A Loterie Nationale," December 24, 1992, pp. 2–4.

Le Figaro. "FDJ Lottery Operator Sees Turnover Grow," January 19, 1993, p. 50.

The Financial Times of London. "Spanish Charity Locks Horns with Ministry Over Lottery," June 4, 1991, pp. 46–49.

The Financial Times of London. "Berjaya Wins Chinese Contract for Lottery," March 4, 1992, p. 15.

Fleming, Alice. *Something for Nothing.* New York: Delacorte Press, 1978.

Irish Times. "£252.3 Million Sales for Lottery," February 26, 1993, pp. 21–23.

Kant, Immanuel. *Groundwork of the Metaphysic of Morals.* Translated and analyzed by H. J. Paton. New York: Harper & Row, 1964.

Karcher, Alan J. *Lotteries.* New Brunswick, NJ: Transaction Publishers, 1989.

Kingdon, John W. *Agendas, Alternatives, and Public Policies.* Ann Arbor, MI: HarperCollins, 1984.

Ljung, G. M. and G.E.P. Box. "On a Measure of Lack of Fit in Time Series Models." *Biometrika* 65 (297) 1978.

Massachusetts Lottery Commission: A Summary Description, edited by Thomas O'Heir and Eric Turner for the years 1989, 1990, 1991, and 1992, Braintree, MA.

McAllister, Ian and Donley T. Studlar. "Popular Versus Elite Views of Privatization." *Journal of Public Policy* 9 (1989): pp. 125–137.

McGowan, Richard A. "Public Policy Measures and Cigarette Sales: An ARIMA Intervention Analysis" in *Research in Corporate and*

Social Performance and Policy, edited by James Post, Greenwich, CT: JAI Press, 1989.

New York Times. "News Briefs," April 2, 1990, p. B1.

New York Times. Meier, Barry. "Russia's Poor Push Their Luck," November 23, 1992, p. D1.

New York Times. Meier, Barry. "Gifted Russian Youths: Sign Up Here," February 16, 1993, p. D3.

New York Times. Kleinfield, N. R. "Legal Gambling Faces Higher Odds," August 29, 1993, p. E3.

The Observer. "Opposition to National Lottery," July 19, 1992, p. 1.

The Observer. "Britain Takes a £4 Billion Gamble," December 8, 1992, pp. 1–3.

Onkvisit, Sak and John J. Shaw. *Product Life Cycles and Product Management*. Westport, CT: Greenwood Press, 1989.

El Pais. "Authorities Restructure Control of National Lottery," May 31, 1992, p. 28.

Pint, Ellen M. "Nationalization and Privatization." *Journal of Public Policy* 10 (1990): 263–273.

Philadelphia Inquirer. Warner, Susan. "OTB: New Jobs and Promise," February 11, 1993, p. C1.

Philadelphia Inquirer. "Meaningful Learning for Our Students," December 29, 1993, p. A13.

Philadelphia Inquirer. Warner, Susan. "Bally's to Buy Riverfront Property," January 5, 1994, pp. A1–A8.

Press Association Newsfile, "Irish Lottery Sales Top One Billion," December 24, 1992, pp. 24–26.

Press Association Newsfile. "Why Irish Charities Are Smiling," February 3, 1993, p. 47.

Press Association Newsfile. "Community Takes Gamble to Help Jobless," March 30, 1993, p. 21.

Providence Journal. "Keno," January 1, 1993, pp. 59–61.

Reuters Library Report. "Gambling Fever Grips Chinese Party Members, Peasants," February 8, 1988, p. 5.

Rosen, Sam and Desmond Norton. "The Lottery as a Source of Public Revenue," *Taxes*, vol. 44, 1966.

Savas, E. S. *Privatization: The Key to Better Government*. Chatham, NJ: Chatham House, 1987.

Scranton Times. "Area Bus Service Threat," December 23, 1993, pp. 1–2.

South China Morning Post. "Punt on Gambling Stocks Is Safe Bet," February 9, 1993, p. 2.

Sullivan, George. *By Chance a Winner: The History of Lotteries.* New York: Dodd, Mead & Co., 1972.

The Sunday Telegraph. "Lottery Addicts Have Spain in Constant Flutter," May 17, 1992, p. 12.

Time. "Las Vegas, U.S.A.," January 10, 1994, pp. 42–51.

The Times of London. "Spaniards Gamble on Winning 'The Fat One,' " December 22, 1992, p. 31.

USA Today. "Soviet Lotto," October 5, 1991, p. D1.

Vickers, John and George Yarrow, *Privatization: An Economic Analysis.* Cambridge, MA: MIT Press, 1988.

Wall Street Journal. "Albania Finances Olympic Team," March 9, 1992, p. 3.

Warsaw Voice. "Games of Chance: House of Cards," January 19, 1992, pp. 2–5.

World Lottery Almanac. "Breakdown of Lottery Sales Worldwide," Terri LaFleur Publications, New York, 1993.

Xinhua General Overseas News. "China's Nationwide Donation-collecting Campaign for Flood Victims Continues," July 14, 1991, p. 1.

Xinhua General Overseas News. "Sports Lottery," June 5, 1992, p. 3.

Zorn, Kurt C. "The Lottery: Its Economic Effects," *Indiana Business Review* 63 (April 1988).

Index

About the Author

RICHARD McGOWAN is Associate Professor and Assistant
Provost for Academic Affairs, University of Scranton. His primary
focus of research is the interactions between business and public
policy processes, especially related to the tobacco, alcohol, oil, and
steel industries.

ISBN 0-89930-859-7

90000>

EAN

9 780899 308593

HARDCOVER BAR CODE